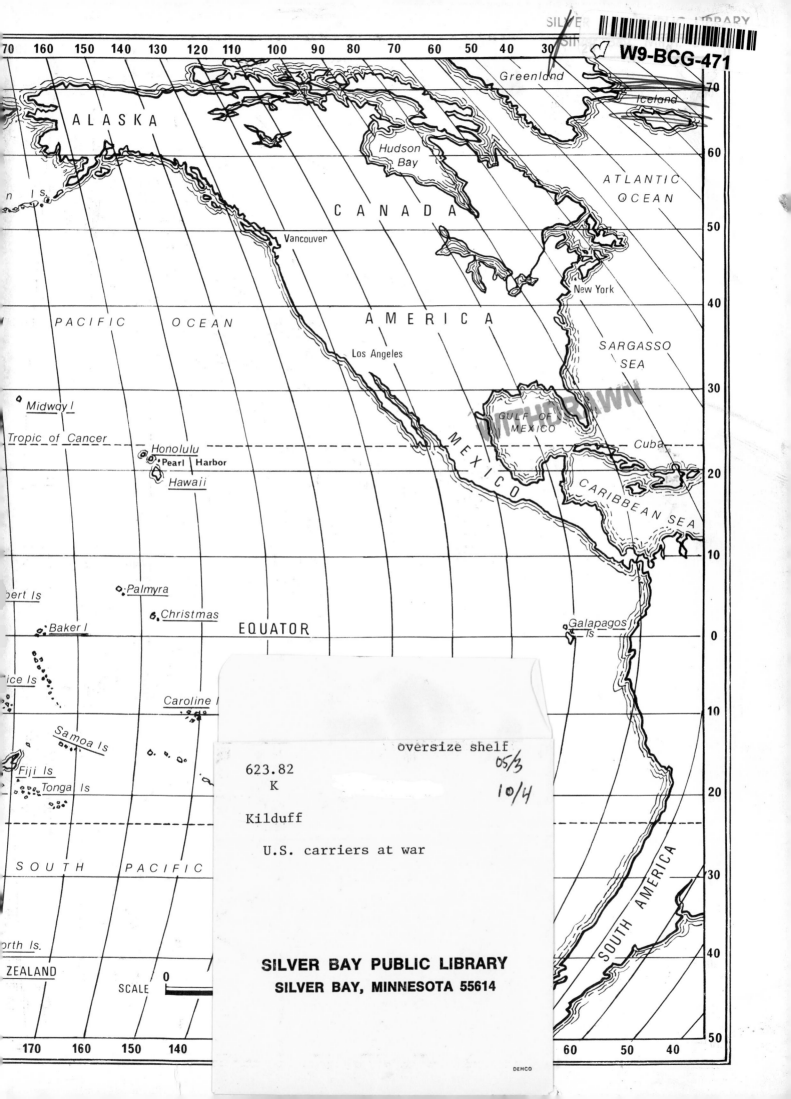

# US Carriers
## at war

# US Carriers
## at war

## Peter Kilduff

STACKPOLE BOOKS

623.82
K

# Contents

# Introduction

The first American aircraft carrier was commissioned on 20 March 1922. Although US Navy pilots had taken off from and landed aboard specially-rigged platforms on other ships prior to World War 1, the Americans' operational use of the aircraft carrier did not begin until USS *Langley* (CV-1) entered service.

USS *Langley* was converted from a prewar fleet collier to an aircraft carrier by adding a 534ft by 64ft wooden flight deck and an aircraft elevator above the superstructure of the onetime coal hauler. Although she was neither very big nor very fast, *Langley* provided the sea-going aircraft platform for the cadre of US naval pilots who went on to prominence in the World War 2 aircraft carrier fleet that became the largest and most effective maritime aircraft strike force in the world.

The Washington Naval Treaty signed on 6 February 1921 prohibited the US Navy from adding a new class of large battlecruisers to its fleet, but did allow the two hulls already laid down to be completed as aircraft carriers. Thus, while USS *Langley* was still being fitted out, the next step in the evolution of American aircraft carriers had already begun. The two ex-battlecruisers converted to aircraft carriers became USS *Lexington* (CV-2) and USS *Saratoga* (CV-3), both commissioned in 1927. 'Lex' and 'Sara', as they were affectionately known, were vast improvements over *Langley*. Their 888ft long flight decks allowed the use of more and larger aircraft, whose take-off run into the wind along the length of the flight deck was aided by the new carriers' greater speed.

USS *Ranger* (CV-4), the first American ship built as an aircraft carrier from the keel up, joined the fleet in 1934. During the next seven years the American carrier force slowly grew by four additional ships: USS *Yorktown* (CV-5), USS *Enterprise* (CV-6), USS *Wasp* (CV-7) and USS *Hornet* (CV-8).

The second world wide war was already in progress when, on 3 July 1940, the US Navy was authorised to order 11 new aircraft carriers. These were to be the largest such ships in the American inventory and they were authorised to meet the clearly growing threat of American involvement in the war. Indeed, the carrier-launched sneak attack on the American base at Pearl Harbor, Hawaii on Sunday 7 December 1941 was more than adequate proof of the need for a large, highly-mobile aircraft strike force that could operate in the great expanse of the Pacific Ocean.

Although the United States lost four of her seven operational carriers within the first year of her involvement in World War 2, the promise of ultimate victory existed in the new class of large-deck carriers that would follow USS *Essex* (CV-9). Displacing 36,380ton fully loaded and with flight decks either 872ft or 888ft long, the 'Essex' class ships became the big. fast carriers that played a major role in the American military success in the Pacific. None of them were ever sunk and, indeed, the four US carriers lost early in the war were remembered in the names of the later 'Essex' class ships *Yorktown* (CV-10), *Hornet* (CV-12), *Lexington* (CV-16) and *Wasp* (CV-18).

Moreover, while Japanese wartime production of aircraft carriers was minimal, American shipyards completed 17 'Essex' class CVs, nine light carriers that were designated CVLs and 120 small-deck escort carriers known as CVEs, of which the latter were produced for both the US Navy and the Royal Navy.

A small number of American aircraft carriers, mostly CVEs, were deployed in the Atlantic and were quite successful in finding and sinking German submarines. For the most part, however, the 'carrier war' was fought in the Pacific, where the carriers were alternately attached to Task Force 38 or Task Force 58. The enemy often thought they were two entirely different forces, but the designation was applied when overall command was given to either Adm William F. Halsey, Jr (Third Fleet) or Adm Raymond A. Spruance (Fifth Fleet).

Many of the 'Essex' class carriers continued to serve long after World War 2. Indeed, this writer gained an early appreciation of and deep affection for those magnificent ships and their intrepid pilots and aircrewmen during a tour of duty 20 years ago aboard USS *Lake Champlain* (CVS-39), the last of the straight-deck, open-bow 'Essex' class carriers.

Thus, to produce a book on aircraft carrier operations has been one of this writer's long-time ambitions. By no means has this been a singular undertaking and it is only thanks to many friends and associates that it has actually been possible. Foremost among these has been Vice-Adm William D. Houser, USN (Ret), former Deputy Chief of Naval Operations (Air Warfare). He has always been willing to help and, very important for a writer-historian, provide contacts and sources for further information. To Bill Houser goes a special debt of gratitude.

The naval establishment has always been helpful in the course of this writer's various projects, but special thanks are due to Clark Van Vleet of the Naval Aviation History Office and to Bob Carlisle and Lyn M. Sundberg of the Navy's Office of Information.

Chief among my helpful historian colleagues has been Dr Brian P. Flanagan, a fellow editor of *The Cross & Cockade Journal*. His fine eye for detail and his incisive critique of the manuscript were helpful. Bob Lawson and Lt Pete Clayton of the editorial staff of *The Hook*, the quarterly publication of The Tailhook Association, came through in a pinch as this work drew to a close and I am very grateful to them.

On the research side, R.S. ('Steve') Fletcher proved himself to be an astute naval aviation historian and I sincerely appreciate all of the help he provided from his own substantial archives. Deep thanks are also extended for the assistance provided by Bob Mikesh of the National Air & Space Museum, Elayne P. Bendel of the

Douglas Aircraft Company, H.J. ('Schoney') Schonenberg of Grumman Aerospace, and Gene Wright of MPB Corporation.

My great regard and admiration goes to the men whose experiences are recounted in this book. Special thanks, therefore, are accorded to: Rear-Adm George L. Cassell, USN (Ret); Rear-Adm Maxwell F. Leslie, USN (Ret); Dr Norman A. Sterrie; Capt Gaylord Brown, USN (Ret); Cdr Maynard Furney, USN (Ret); and Jim Ean of the Intrepid Museum Foundation. My gratitude is also extended to Capt Frank DeLorenzo of the *Association of Naval Aviation* for his help in lining up interview subjects for this book.

Saving the best for last, I accord special thanks to my wife, Judy, who has listened to this project since the day it was conceived and whose own interest in history has served as the ideal sounding board for the development of my first aircraft carrier book. Her encouragement and perception are appreciated in words beyond measure.

New Britain, Connecticut          *Peter Kilduff*

---

# Abbreviations

**AA**   anti-aircraft
**ACA Report**   Air Combat Activity Report
**ACRM(A)**   (Acting) Chief Aviation Radioman
**ACV (formerly AVG)**   auxiliary aircraft carrier
**AGC**   Air Group Commander
**AK**   matériel transport ship
**AMM1c**   Aviation Machinist's Mate 1st Class
**AOM2c**   Aviation Ordnanceman 2nd Class
**AP**   troop transport ship
**ARM1c**   Aviation Radioman 1st Class
**ASP**   anti-submarine patrol
**AVG**   aircraft escort vessel
**BB**   battleship
**BuNo**   Bureau of Aeronautics serial number
**CA**   heavy cruiser
**CAP**   combat air patrol
**CL**   light cruiser

**CV**   fleet-type aircraft carrier
**CVE (formerly ACV)**   escort aircraft carrier
**CVL**   light aircraft carrier
**DD**   destroyer
**DE**   destroyer escort
**LSO**   Landing Signal Officer
**NAS**   Naval Air Station
**OA**   fleet oiler (ship)
**RM3c**   Radioman 3rd Class
**VB**   bombing squadron
**VBF**   fighter bombing squadron
**VC**   composite squadron
**VF**   fighter squadron
**VF(N)**   night fighter squadron
**VMF**   Marine Corps fighter squadron
**VMSB**   Marine Corps scout bombing squadron
**VOF**   observation fighter squadron
**VS**   scouting squadron
**VT**   torpedo squadron

---

# Enemy Aircraft Code-Names

**Betty**   Mitsubishi G4M and G6M series twin-engine naval attack bomber
**Dinah**   Mitsubishi Ki-46 Army Type 100 twin-engine reconnaissance aircraft
**Frances**   Yokosuka P1Y series twin-engine naval attack bomber
**Frank**   Nakajima Ki-84 Army Type 4 fighter aircraft
**George**   Kawanishi N1K series Navy interceptor
**Hamp**   Mitsubishi A6M3 Navy Type 0 carrier-based fighter Model 32

**Helen**   Nakajima Ki-49 Army Type 100 heavy bomber
**Irving**   Nakajima J1N1 Navy twin-engine or night fighter aircraft
**Jill**   Nakajima B6N Navy carrier-based attack bomber
**Judy**   Yokosuka D4Y Navy carier-based attack bomber
**Kate**   Nakajima B5N Navy Type 97 carrier-based attack bomber
**Nate**   Nakajima Ki-27 Army Type 97 fighter aircraft
**Oscar**   Nakajima Ki-43 Army Type 1 fighter aircraft
**Rufe**   Nakajima A6M2-N Navy Type 2 fighter seaplane
**Tojo**   Nakajima Ki-44 Army Type 2 fighter aircraft
**Tony**   Kawasaki Ki-61 Army Type 3 fighter aircraft
**Val**   Aichi D3A Navy Type 99 carrier-based bomber
**Zeke**   Mitsubishi A6M series Navy Type 0 carrier-based fighter aircraft
**Zero**   common name for 'Hamp' and 'Zeke' fighters

# Torpedo Pilot

Naval aircraft had been used to launch torpedoes since the biplane seaplane days of World War 1. However, a new era in US Navy torpedo-carrying aircraft began on 5 October 1937, when torpedo squadron VT-3 received its initial example of the first American carrier-based monoplane designed for that mission, the Douglas TBD-1 Devastator. The following year the new torpedo bombers were supplied to VT-2, VT-5 and VT-6.

The Douglas Devastator is recalled by Dr Norman A. Sterrie, who entered US Navy flight training in October 1939 and received his gold wings in August 1940. A month later he was assigned to VT-2 aboard USS *Lexington* (CV-2), at which time the TBDs were already beginning to show their age. He recalls:

'The TBD was a very easy plane to fly. It was very stable, but slow. We usually operated at speeds of 110-120kts and found the Pratt & Whitney engines to be extremely reliable and, according to our mechanics, quite easy to maintain. By 1941, however, the airplanes were corroding badly and after all flights we had to perform special inspections through all the key stress areas. We also had to be careful about where we walked and where we placed stress on the aircraft. The aluminium was deteriorating so badly due to the corrosive action of the sea over many months of service that, on more than one occasion, crewmen had put a foot through the fuselage as the aluminium turned to powder.

'In the air, the TBD was very forgiving, although there were limitations to the Gs that could be applied. There was no "pulling out of a dive" because we never dove those planes. Before the war VT-2 spent a considerable amount of time in practising high-level bombing, using the then secret Norden bombsight. But that had no application for VT-2 once we got into war. We didn't really begin to use torpedoes as we were supposed to do until the action of the Battle of the Coral Sea.'

USS *Lexington* was transporting 18 Vought SB2U Vindicators of Marine Corps scout bombing squadron VMSB-231 to Midway Island when the Japanese attacked Pearl Harbor. That mission was abruptly altered when, at 0758hrs on 7 December 1941, the carrier was ordered to 'intercept and destroy enemy believed retreating on a course between Pearl Harbor and Jaluit. Intercept and destroy.'

Dr Sterrie remembers:

'We were off Midway, ready to discharge the Marine aircraft when word of the attack came. We had already planned to carry out exercises that day, so the only changes required were to replace practice ammunition with service ammunition and to load up with bombs. We were ready for war at the time and, in fact, had been for months before that.

'Initially, we headed south of Oahu, searching for the Japanese strike force, which had long since gone north. In retrospect, that was probably fortunate for us, as we would not have been able to cope with that entire force on our own. We returned to Pearl Harbor several days after the attack and left shortly thereafter, spending our time until the Battle of the Coral Sea on two extended trips down into the area near Australia.

'Shortly after we left Pearl Harbor, my wingman and I were on a flight near Johnston Island, south west of Oahu, when we spotted a Japanese submarine on the surface. While we attempted to investigate the nationality of the

submarine, we suddenly found ourselves being shot at by one of the sub's guns. The submarine made a hasty dive before we could return the fire. I don't know whatever happened to the submarine, but I doubt that the depth charges we dropped did much damage; at least there was no oil slick or debris to indicate a hit. In any case, the submarine had already gone under by the time we reached it.'

Since the Japanese naval base on Truk, in the Caroline Islands, could easily be the staging area for a strike against Australia, the US Navy had to maintain a deterrent force in the Coral Sea. Thus, USS *Lexington* became part of Task Force 11 and the Flagship of Vice-Adm Wilson Brown, the task force commander. On 20 February 1942 the Japanese made their first attempt to sink the *Lexington*. Attempting to duplicate their success of 10 December 1941, when land-based bombers sunk the battleship HMS *Prince of Wales* and the battlecruiser HMS *Repulse*, the Japanese sent a land-based bomber force after USS *Lexington*. Fighter squadron VF-2, led by Lt-Cdr John S. ('Jimmie') Thach, proved the value of carrier-based air support by shooting down 16 of the 18

Japanese bombers. In one epic portion of the aerial combat, Lt(jg) Edward H. ('Butch') O'Hare shot down five of the marauders, for which he was subsequently advanced two ranks to Lieutenant Commander and awarded the Medal of Honor.

*Lexington*'s torpedo aircraft went on the offensive on 10 March, when they went after targets in Salamaua and Lae on the island of New Guinea. Of special interest were two excellent airfields that had been built for New Guinea Airways but that now served Japanese forces attacking Port Moresby on the other side of the island. Salamaua and Lae also served as defensive points on either edge of a tropical lagoon that accommodated both supply and combat ships. Cdr Bill Ault, *Lexington*'s Air Group Commander, assigned the lagoon to VT-2. As Sterrie recalls:

'Prior to the raid Cdr Ault went to Port Moresby for a briefing. He was given maps and information about the enemy, both of which were rather sparse. The mimeographed maps that were handed out appeared to come from a *National Geographic* magazine or some other non-military source of geographical information about New Guinea. Of course, we had never flown over that island and did not know what it was like there, so we had to rely heavily on the maps. One particular mountain pass, for example, was listed as being about 8,000ft or higher and, since we had never carried torpedoes to such an altitude, there was some question as to whether we would be able to make it over the top.

'We proceeded up the pass as a full Air Group and it soon became very apparent that the torpedo planes, at least, were not going to make it. Just when it seemed that all was lost, we flipped over on our sides to backtrack and start over. We did make it the second time, but we certainly wondered when that cross-over was going to take place because, as I recall, we were very close to the ground at that point. We actually saw some of the native shacks right under our wingtips. Once we got over the pass, we proceeded up to Salamaua and Lae, where we took on freighter elements and some protecting ships. I don't recall that the anti-aircraft fire was particularly heavy, but it was bad enough to cause the loss of one or two of our dive bombers.* No torpedo bombers were lost during that attack.

The *Lexington*-launched raids against Salamaua and Lae were successful. The fighters, dive bombers and torpedo bombers gave the port facilities and the ships in the lagoon a good working over. For that day's work there were 14 presentations of the Navy Cross, America's second highest naval decoration for valour. Eight *Lexington* pilots and aircrew received the Distinguished Flying Cross.

The Navy Cross citation for Dr Norman Sterrie, then an Ensign, reads: 'For distinguished service in the line of his profession as a pilot of a scouting [sic] squadron, when, on 10 March 1942, in enemy waters, he participated in a vigorous and determined dive-bombing attack, in the face of heavy anti-aircraft fire, on enemy ships, and as a result of this attack at least one ship was sunk.'

*During this engagement, Cdr William B. Ault flew in a Douglas SBD, one of the 18 SBD-2 and 3 aircraft assigned to VB-2. Other dive bombers from that unit were led by Lt-Cdr Weldon L. Hamilton, squadron commander. Lt-Cdr Robert E. Dixon, commanding officer of VS-2, was part of another group of the 18 SBD-2 and -3 aircraft assigned to that unit. Lt-Cdr James H. Brett, Jr was in charge of the 12 TBD-1 aircraft of VT-2. 22 F4F-3s were allotted to VF-2.

*Below:* TBD-1 in wartime markings over the Pacific. /US Navy

After the Salamaua-Lae strike, USS *Lexington* returned to Pearl Harbor for a three-week maintenance period. She put to sea again on 15 April and joined USS *Yorktown* (CV-5) in becoming the key elements of Task Force 17 under the command of Rear-Adm Frank Jack Fletcher. Due to strict radio silence then in force, Adm Fletcher believed *Lexington* was still refuelling at sea, when, on 4 May, he ordered *Yorktown* to attack the Japanese base at Tulagi in the Solomon Islands. That incident marked the beginning of the Battle of the Coral Sea, as, the next night, the two 25,675ton Japanese fleet aircraft carriers *Shokaku* and *Zuikaku* entered the Coral Sea on a southerly heading that would bring them in contact with *Lexington* and *Yorktown*.

The battle began at 0610hrs on 7 May, when the two Japanese carriers launched 18 Mitsubishi A6M5 'Zeke' fighters, 36 Aichi D3A 'Val' dive bombers and 24 Mitsubishi B5M 'Kate' torpedo bombers. Failing to find the American carriers, the Japanese aircraft pounced on the fleet oiler USS *Neosho* (AO-23) and the destroyer USS *Sims* (DD-409). Both ships were lost.

A short time later, however, aircraft from the American carriers found the 11,262ton Japanese light carrier *Shoho* and her escorts and attacked them. The Americans sank the *Shoho* – the first Japanese aircraft carrier to be sunk in World War 2 – whose demise was noted by VS-2's commanding officer, Lt-Cdr Robert E. Dixon, in the famous message: 'Scratch one flattop.' The next day the main Japanese carrier force would enter combat in the first naval engagement in history carried out entirely by aircraft, with the opposing ships never in sight of each other.

Torpedo bombers proved to be an important weapon in the Battle of the Coral Sea, in spite of some inherent weaknesses, as recalled by Dr Norman Sterrie:

'We again carried torpedoes during the action in the Coral Sea, which is what we were really meant to do. However, there were very real limitations on our equipment. We had older planes that were slow and functioned at a very different level compared to the more modern fighter and dive bomber aircraft in our Air Group. Since coordination was the name of the game, this created quite an altitude difference, to say nothing of speed. So, coordination was not always of the best. We depended heavily on line of sight and, with any disturbance of the cloud cover or any adverse weather condition, the coordinated attack was a very difficult one to carry out.

'Operations during the first day of the Coral Sea battle [7 May] were well coordinated and we had good fighter protection. However, during the second day coordination was markedly lacking. Inter-squadron communications were poor – probably due to radio silence – and there was virtually no coordination among the separate squadrons during the attack itself. Fortunately, we in VT-2 were not under fighter attack at that time. I believe the bombers and fighters absorbed most of that action.

'I do feel, however, that we were at a very high level of proficiency. The pilots were extremely well trained, but limited very much by the equipment. The torpedoes had to be dropped at very slow speed and were inconsistent and easily damaged. This was not a very practical or effective way of conducting a torpedo attack. The distance the torpedoes had to be launched from the target for an effective attack was much too short for the speed at which we could be expected to drop them.'

Vice-Adm Takeo Takagi, commander of the Carrier Striking Force that was part of the overall task force charged with the invasion of Port Moresby, launched his aircraft at about 0700hrs on 8 May. He sent 18 fighters, 33 dive bombers and 18 torpedo bombers out after the two American carriers. Meanwhile, his counterpart, Rear-Adm Fletcher, had ordered the launching of 18 *Lexington* scout aircraft at 0625hrs. At 0930, Lt-Cdr R.E. Dixon of VS-2 confirmed an earlier scouting report about the location of the two Japanese carriers. As that message was coming in, *Lexington* was launching nine of VF-2's F4Fs, 22 SBDs from VS-2 and VB-2 and all 12 of VT-2's TBDs. While the *Yorktown*'s Air

*Below:* Japanese aircraft carrier *Shokaku* under attack during the Battle of the Coral Sea./*US Navy*

*Bottom:* Japanese aircraft carrier *Ryukaku* under attack during the Battle of the Coral Sea./*US Navy*

Group went after the Japanese carrier *Zuikaku*, Cdr W.B. Ault led the *Lexington* aircraft toward the *Shokaku*. Navigational difficulties caused a number of *Lexington*'s aircraft to return to the carrier, but at 1140hrs, Cdr Ault directed six Wildcats, four Dauntlesses and VT-2's 12 Devastators against their target.

Dr Sterrie's initial recollection of that attack appeared in *Queen of the Flat-tops* by Stanley Johnston (E.P. Dutton and Co, Inc; 1942) and noted the events as follows:

'The clouds ranged from 2,000 to 6,000ft and after the preparatory examination of the enemy disposition the squadron leader dived for the attack position.

'We fanned out and headed in at high speed. This time we were recognised and met by heavy anti-aircraft fire. And a lot of Jap fighters showed up but did not push their attacks home.

'Group Commander Bill Ault's four planes dived simultaneously with our torpedo run. All concentrated on the carrier.

'The Jap [carrier] went into a tight constant turn when attacked. By the time it was my turn she already was smoking, showing evidence of having been hit. I dropped my "fish" on her starboard quarter 75ft above the water, 500yd out. At the time I was being subjected to heavy anti-aircraft fire and attack from a fighter.

'As I was joining up with the main group, one of the boys who had not let go of his fish [Lt-Cdr J.H. Brett, Jr] said he was going to attack a cruiser. So I accompanied him making a dummy run to assist in absorbing the ship's anti-aircraft fire.'

Some 37 years after the event, Dr Sterrie added to that description by noting:
'I remember going in the second time with the other pilot, who was our squadron commander.

Most of all I recall flying through slipstreams of shells, none of which, fortunately, had my name on it.

'On our return flight we crossed the path of the Japanese group that had attacked our ships. Since we were both at extreme range, that group did nothing but make a slight gesture toward us. They, of course, knew nothing about what they would face on their return.* I suspect their fuel load was rather meagre in terms of getting back to their carriers in recoverable condition. Our fuel situation was critical, too. I watched "Tiny" Thornhill, truly an outstanding officer and a warm and wonderful person, go in. As the squadron's Engineering Officer, I had ordered accurate fuel consumption measurements taken on all previous flights and I knew that Tiny's plane was a "gas hog". We had not been able to correct that engine deficiency and he was well aware of this. It seemed that we were always functioning at just a little bit beyond our usually acceptable range. We never saw that fine officer again.

'On returning to our fleet we came under anti-aircraft attack by our own forces. They, of course, had been under a very intense and deadly Japanese attack and, since we were unable to make the recognition turn to indicate we were friendly, we took quite a bombardment coming in. We had not made that manoeuvre because we feared we would not have enough fuel to see us back aboard the carrier. Fortunately, the attack on us was called off before anybody was hurt.

*The carrier *Shokaku* was so badly damaged during the attack that, although she managed to elude a fatal stroke that would send her to the bottom, she was unable either to launch or to recover aircraft. Hence, her sister ship, *Zuikaku*, had to jettison damaged aircraft she recovered in order to make room for recoverable aircraft from *Shokaku*.

*Below:* Smouldering flight deck of USS *Lexington* after Japanese air attack during the Battle of the Coral Sea./*US Navy*

*Above:* VT-2's Douglas TBD-1 Devastators.
*/Douglas Aircraft Company*

'After we got back aboard the *Lexington*, most of us felt very sick that Bill Ault had been lost during our engagement with the Japanese carriers.* By the standard of the day, people of his seniority were usually regarded as rather old beside us young kids. Promotions had not been very good in the years prior to the war and many outstanding men were sent to the fleet for leadership experience. Unfortunately, Cdr Ault never survived.'

While the aircraft from *Lexington* and *Yorktown* were attacking the two Japanese aircraft carriers, the two American ships came under an intensive bombing and torpedo attack from enemy aircraft. The 19,900ton, 741ft-long *Yorktown* was smaller and more manoeuvrable than USS

*Cdr William B. Ault, his three comrades and their two fighter escorts were attacked by a force of more than 20 enemy fighter aircraft. Just before ditching, Cdr Ault radioed that his SBD was badly shot up, his rear gunner was severely wounded and that he himself was wounded. He apparently perished at sea. The destroyer USS *Ault* (DD-698) honoured his memory and Ault Field in his native state of Washington was also named in his honour; it is still in service.

*Lexington*, which displaced 40,000ton fully loaded and was 888ft long. Consequently, *Yorktown* was better able to make the radical 30kt turns necessary to evade the Japanese attackers. The less agile *Lexington* was struck at 1120hrs by a torpedo on the forward port side and, a moment later, by another one farther aft on the same side. Several bombs also hit *Lexington*, but did relatively little damage. Indeed, most of the damage had been repaired and a seven-degree list corrected when, at 1247hrs, a massive internal explosion rocked the ship. Leaking gasoline vapours ignited by a spark from a generator caused the explosion that sealed the fate of the US Navy's second aircraft carrier. A raging fire broke out and set off other explosions.

Despite the mounting damage to the carrier, Dr Sterrie notes that he was able to make one final landing aboard USS *Lexington*:
'We came aboard a ship that was listing and smoking heavily but that was still underway and into the wind. My plane came to rest on an elevator and as I stepped out of the plane I was lifted about two feet into the air as a major explosion took place below decks.

'The ship was in bad shape and we spent the rest of the afternoon on the aft deck, inhaling the smoke. We could not possibly have gotten off to the other carrier [USS *Yorktown*] because our fuel supplies had been shut off. And I wasn't sure there would have been enough room to accommodate us on the other carrier without shoving their own planes over the side.

'After taking in all that black smoke for several hours and being quite aware that we were ultimately going to have to leave the ship, we were quite relieved when the "abandon ship" order came. Many men slid down ropes into the sea. I dropped the life raft from a plane overboard and then watched it be swamped by survivors below, who pushed off without me. I went to another plane, got another life raft and teamed with one of my buddies to hold it until I could get down, as well. We had many people around our life raft, and one or two inside, and managed to stay afloat until we were finally taken aboard the cruiser USS *Indianapolis* (CA-35). We were subsequently transferred to a destroyer that took us over to Tonga Island.'

The agony of 'Lady Lex' lasted until early on the morning of 9 May, when the destroyer USS *Phelps* (DD-360) fired four torpedoes into the blazing hull to sink it, even though it was unlikely the Japanese would have been able to capture it as a war prize. The survivors of VT-2 were subsequently reunited. Half of the squadron personnel were sent to the Fiji Islands and the other half to New Caledonia, where, Dr Sterrie notes:
'They instructed the then US Army Air Corps squadrons in torpedo warfare. After the Battle of the Coral Sea and surely after the Battle of Midway there was little left of any force that could handle torpedo warfare. There was a quick attempt to make torpedo pilots out of the Martin

*Above:* Crew is forced to abandon USS *Lexington.*/US Navy

*Right:* Explosions aboard USS *Lexington* mark her final agony. /US Navy

B-26 Marauder pilots. Although we flew "second-seat" on many practice missions, we TBD pilots did not actually check out in the B-26. I doubt there would have been time for that and I think that the young US Army Air Corps pilots needed all of the flight time they could get for themselves.'

Despite the loss of USS *Lexington*, American forces are generally credited with being victorious in the Battle of the Coral Sea. They achieved the primary objective of halting the invasion of Port Moresby and thereby averted the most serious threat of a subsequent invasion

of Australia. For his role in inflicting severe damage on the Japanese aircraft carrier *Shokaku*, Norman Sterrie was awarded the Gold Star in lieu of a second Navy Cross.

The survivors of VT-2 were eventually returned to the United States and posted to other duties. While most aircrewmen from the ill-fated *Lexington* were sent to training squadrons, to give the incoming forces the benefit of their combat experience, Dr Sterrie was assigned to a West Coast operational unit, VT-12. That squadron was quickly decommissioned and he was transferred to NAS

Quonset Point, Rhode Island, where a new squadron, VT-16, was being formed under the command of Cdr Robert Isely. That squadron was to be an element of Air Group 16 assigned to the new USS *Lexington* (CV-16), which was originally laid down as USS *Cabot*, but renamed in honour of the carrier lost in the Battle of the Coral Sea.

US Navy ships at that time were painted with rust-resistance primer, a bluish base coat and then a blue-grey camouflage coat. The new USS *Lexington* was pressed into action so quickly that she arrived in the Pacific in August of 1943 minus the standard camouflage, thus being the only

carrier in that theatre of operations without camouflage. Consequently, *Lexington* was nicknamed 'the blue ghost of the Pacific'.

During his second tour of combat duty Norman Sterrie flew the Grumman TBF-1 Avenger and the General Motors license-built variant, the TBM-1. He recalls:
'There was no real difference [between the two variants]. The TBM was a later model and certainly had 10 years of improvements over the old TBD Devastator. In itself, the TBM was not as fast an aircraft as we might have expected but in direct speed we gained about 40kts over the TBD. With the TBM we also had the ability to

*Below:* The new USS *Lexington* (CV-16) at sea./*US Navy*

*Bottom:* Another photograph of the new USS *Lexington* (CV-16). /*US Navy*

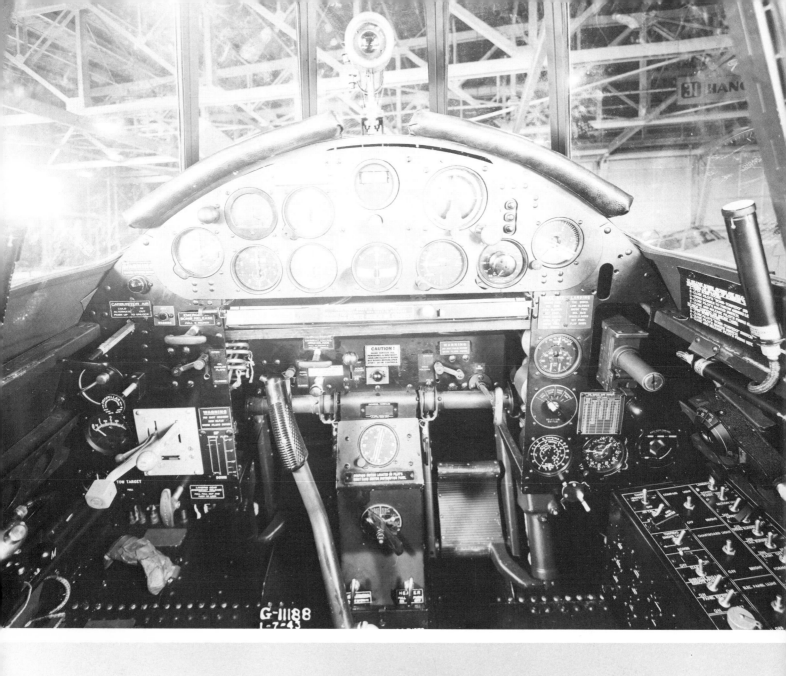

glide bomb and exert certain Gs that the TBD would never have withstood. The armament was enclosed in a bomb bay, in contrast to the exterior loading on the TBD. The TBM's engine was certainly much more powerful and the Avenger's instrumentation was much better; we had a radar altimeter that gave a direct, accurate reading.

'Initially, Bob Isely and I flew the first two planes with radar, which was quite an improvement over the TBD, which had no radar at all. The TBD's homing equipment was reassuring, but not all that efficient. It relied on the "Y-E/Z-B" system, based on a signal broadcast in a certain area that allowed us to know what segment of an operating radius we were in and to compute our direction back to the ship, provided, of course, the equipment was turned on aboard both the aircraft and the ship's transmitter.

'We never could have carried out the type of warfare that was demanded of us during later actions in a plane such as the TBD. It was principally the capacity of the TBM to function at a considerably higher speed and, although not able to dive bomb, certainly be able to glide bomb and take considerably more stress. The TBD was probably a more manoeuvrable airplane, but we didn't really require manoeuvrability. The TBM, on the other hand, was a very rugged aircraft and could take quite a beating and still fly.'

*Left:* Cockpit of Grumman TBF-1 Avenger./*Grumman Aerospace*

*Below left:* TBF-1 launched from 'Essex' class carrier./*US Navy*

*Below:* Wreckage of a 'Zeke' shot down during Marianas campaign. /*US Air Force*

Air Group 16, under the command of Cdr E.M. Snowden, received its first combat mission assignment shortly after arriving at Pearl Harbor. On 18 September 1943 the combined Air Group hit Japanese positions on Tarawa in the Gilbert Islands group on the eastern perimeter of the Japanese expansion in the Pacific. As Norman Sterrie recalls, it was an unusual – and often harrowing – baptism under fire for the new carrier-based squadrons aboard *Lexington*:

'Usually, such attacks were carried out over a two-day period, but the Tarawa raid was a one-day action. We had planned to night-launch to arrive over the target at dawn as a model for future attacks. However, the timing was thrown off. We had not practised night time formation join-ups as a group, or, if we had, everything fell apart for this particular mission. The whole Air Group went in in groups of one to six aircraft and I don't think any single squadron was complete. It was pretty much an individual affair.

'All of the lights were out and, with a hundred planes in the air, we were probably a greater menace to ourselves than the Japanese installations below. At night it always looks as if all the fire is coming right at you – and there was plenty of fire early that morning. Miraculously, nobody was killed as we all flew around in the dark in a very disorganised fashion. There was a lot of radio contact but it was meaningless, announcing that another plane was going down into a dive even though nobody knew which direction or where that action was taking place. Finally, each pilot managed to release his bombs and was glad to get out of there.

'As we returned to Pearl Harbor to regroup for the real Tarawa landings, which were to come later [20 November], we spent a considerable time on the basics of night formation and night time join-up exercises. Our involvement in that later operation was not great. The Marines sent their own pilots over Tarawa and we were sent north to cover Makin Island to make sure that no reinforcements were brought down to Tarawa.'

Prior to the actual invasion of Tarawa, however, Air Group 16 had a score to settle with the Japanese, who had successfully wrested the

Wake Island outpost from the US Marines on 23 December 1941. On 5 and 6 October, Air Group 16 struck Wake Island in part of a continuing series of raids that lasted throughout most of the Pacific War.

VT-16's first losses came during operations to cover the landings in the Gilbert Islands, from 19 to 24 November 1943. However, they were not combat losses. As Dr Sterrie points out: 'There was a large weather system to the north of Tarawa and penetrating this system necessitated instrument formation flying. We had had no practice in that type of flying, since, I suspect, that would have been dangerous to do even under practice conditions. We had received individual instrument training just prior to going to the Pacific, but taking an entire squadron into foul weather on instrument conditions was not part of our experience.

'However, that's just what we were required to do on the first day of the Tarawa action. We entered the weather front in formation, maintaining our distance by radar. Unfortunately, I came out with one less plane, losing Norm White and his crew.'

A little more than two weeks later the new *Lexington* felt the sting of enemy torpedo aircraft during operations off Kwajalein Atoll in the Marshall Islands. Just prior to Air Group 16's launch a Nakajima B5N 'Kate' slipped through the carrier's defensive network and, as Dr Sterrie recalls: 'In a flash he flew right over us, along with his bomb, which crashed into the water just ahead of the ship. Our ship was particularly vulnerable at that point, as all of our planes were fuelled, loaded with bombs and ready for take-off.'

Under a full moon that evening, however, a coordinated torpedo attack by Mitsubishi G4M1 'Betty' bombers had more success. The attack began at 1925hrs and, at 2332, a torpedo struck the *Lexington* and disabled her steering mechanism. The carrier was forced into a tight circular course, Dr Sterrie remembers. 'While we went around and around, a destroyer was left with us. The rest of the fleet took off. Fortunately, the enemy was not aware of our circumstances, or, if they were, they were unable to follow up. Although we did suffer losses during that action, it is to the great credit of the ship's company personnel that the rudder assembly was put back into working order and we were able to limp back to Pearl Harbor.'

Air Group 16 was off-loaded in Hawaii and the *Lexington* sailed for the Bremerton, Washington navy yard, where repairs were made. The carrier did not return to Pearl Harbor until 28 February 1944. With Air Group 16 back aboard, *Lexington* set out for the new advance base of operations at Majuro Atoll in the Marshall Islands. There, on 8 March, Vice-Adm Marc Mitscher, Commander of Task Force 58, shifted his flag aboard *Lexington*, where he remained until October.

Operating from Majuro, *Lexington* led Task Force 58 on a series of raids designed to increasingly diminish the Japanese forward area. On 18 March, Air Group 16 hit Mille Atoll, on the southern end of the Marshall Islands, to consolidate the American position in that island chain. On 22 March, the ship departed Majuro to hit targets on Palau, east of the Philippines.

Before the Palau operation even got under way, however, Norman Sterrie had a horrifying experience:

'While I was testing my machine guns as I headed from Majuro out to the ship just before departure, one of the guns blew up. The explosion set fire to a nearby hydraulic line and burned out a sizeable section of the wing, just aft of the fuel tanks. I ordered the gunner and the radar operator to bail out. Then, as I got out on the wing to bail out, I noticed that the fire seemed to be going out, probably because all of the hydraulic fluid had burned up.

'The plane was still maintaining level flight, so I climbed back in and did manage to bring it back to Majuro. I did not alter the airspeed or test for any kind of stall point. There was a very long runway at Majuro, used by the B-24s, and it should have been able to take any speed that I

*Below: Lexington*-based SBD passes over Japanese aircraft carrier under attack during the Battle of the Philippine Sea./*US Navy*

*Bottom:* Aircraft are examined for combat damage once back aboard USS *Lexington.*/*US Navy*

*Bottom inset:* Lt Norman A. Sterrie in the cockpit of his TBF-1 aboard USS *Lexington.* /*Dr Norman Sterrie*

*Left:* After 28 June 1943, US Navy aircraft such as these Grumman F4F-4 Wildcats had the national insignia made more prominent by the addition of white rectangular bars at either side, with the whole insignia bordered in red. On 4 September 1943, the red border was removed./*US Navy*

*This picture:* SBDs of VB-16 go after targets during invasion of Truk./*US Navy*

*Right:* Trio of SBD Dauntlesses patrol the Pacific./*US Navy*

had. Fortunately, the wheels dropped by gravity and I was able to land the plane. It was probably one of the fastest landings one of those planes had ever made, as I never touched the throttle because I knew it would fly at the speed at which it was going and I was afraid any weakening of the main strut or change of the airflow over the damaged area might re-ignite a fire aft of the fuel tank in the wing.

'I managed to pick up another plane. It was barely flyable and the engine had to be changed before the airplane could be used on the Palau raid. We were not well endowed with spares on these forays, so every plane was very important.

'There were over 30 ships in the harbour at Palau and I gather there must have been some advance knowledge of this concentration of shipping. After we were under way and we were told what our mission would be, we were given instructions by an expert in mine warefare. He told us we would be mining the harbour at Palau, which had two narrow entrances, and that this had to be done with great precision. The six planes under my command would drop the mines, while Bob Isely took his half of the squadron in as glide bombers.

'Our mission was to work with another Air Group's TBMs to bottle up the harbour. Fighters from both Air Groups accompanied us and, fortunately, we were not attacked by enemy fighters. We had to fly a steady course at a certain speed to ensure an accurate distribution of the mines. The timing was very precise, with the mines being released in sequence along the path of the harbour inlet.

'During the second attack of that day [30 March] we were armed with 2,000lb bombs. Much of the shipping had already been destroyed in the harbour, but I selected one of the remaining ships and did manage to plant a 2,000lb into the middle of it. It sank almost immediately.

'This was our first use of skip-bombing. We approached the target at very high speed, just clearing the masthead of the ship involved. Here the danger was that the bomb would "skip" on the water and follow the plane along, but, luckily, that did not happen.

'During this mission we lost Ens L. Curry, who was flying the plane behind mine. One of the advantages of being in the lead plane was that, while they probably shot at you, they were more likely able to pick off the plane behind. This had happened on a number of occasions. Also, the planes behind the leader were not always at liberty to go through the manoeuvring that the lead plane could do. After he was hit, Curry managed to glide into a reef area on the periphery of the Palau islands. A submarine managed to pick up one of the survivors, who, while under enemy fire, waded out to where the submarine could retrieve him.'

After completing the raid on Palau, Air Group 16 hit Woleai in the western Caroline Islands on 1 April. A brief stopover at Majuro was followed by air operations over Hollandia, Dutch New Guinea in support of US Army landings there on 22 April.

USS *Lexington* was joined with USS *Enterprise* (CV-6) and the light carrier USS *San Jacinto* (CVL-30) to deploy as Task Group 58.3 on 6 June 1944 in preparation for the invasion of the Mariana Islands. On 11 June, the first day of Air Group 16's operations, VT-16 was split and given two targets on Saipan. Half of the squadron, led by Commanding Officer Robert Isely, was assigned to hit enemy gun emplacements at the south end of Aslito Airfield on Saipan. The other half, under the command

*Below:* Carrier-based TBFs are loaded with torpedoes./*US Navy*

*Top:* SBD of VB-16 from new USS *Lexington* en route to mission over the Marianas./*US Navy*

*Above:* Nakajima B5N1 'Kate'. /*US Navy*

of Executive Officer Norman Sterrie, was directed toward gun emplacements west of the vital airfield.

That division of assignments, Dr Sterrie reflects:

'... put Bob Isely's group in a particularly hazardous position. I don't know whether he had the customary fighter sweep ahead of his own flight, but he went into an area that proved to be a real hot spot. The defenders were heavily fortified and quickly shot down two of the six TBMs. It is my understanding that Bob Isely must have gone straight in and was hit in the middle of his dive. Ens R. Delgado, in the other plane, had a chance to bail out, but was shot up while making a parachute descent. Nothing further was ever heard of him.

'There was a tremendous amount of bravery demonstrated in that particular attack. Bob was certainly a brave and aggressive person in pushing home the attack.* Unfortunately, the defenses were much greater than we had expected at that time.'

The attack on Saipan and the subsequent encounter between Task Force 58 and the Japanese First Mobile Fleet led to what most historians regard as the biggest carrier battle of World War 2. Opening on 19 June 1944, the encounter is referred to as The First Battle of the Philippine Sea. The tremendous loss of Japanese aircraft that day has led to acceptance of the sobriquet 'the Marianas Turkey Shoot', which was coined by Cdr Paul D. Buie, skipper of VF-16. Indeed, the *Lexington*-based fighter

*After the Americans captured Saipan, Aslito Airfield became a US Naval Air Station and, on 30 June 1944, was renamed Isely Field in honour of Cdr Robert Isely.

*Above:* Early World War 2 markings for US Navy fighter aircraft are seen in this 10 April 1942 view of two Grumman F4F-3 Wildcats from VF-3. Aircraft have rudder stripes and red centres in the white stars, both of which were discontinued on 15 May 1942. Both aircraft also sport the 'Felix the Cat' squadron insignia and aircraft in foreground (Lt-Cdr John S. Thach, Commanding Officer) shows three kill markings. The other Wildcat was piloted by Lt Edward H. ('Butch') O'Hare, later a prominent fighter ace./*US Navy*

squadron accounted for 45 of the 392 Japanese aircraft brought down during the massive encounter. That figure included the six enemy fighters brought down in as many minutes by VF-16's Lt(jg) Alexander Vraciu, then the US Navy's leading ace.

Not content with devastating the Japanese carrier-based air strength, Vice-Adm Mitscher wanted to hit the enemy carriers themselves and thereby break the back of Japanese naval aviation. The enemy's First Mobile Fleet was spotted at 1540hrs – three hours before sunset – on 20 June. Adm Mitscher deliberated the situation and then sent this message to the carriers of Task Force 58: 'Expect to launch everything we have, probably have to recover at night.' The primary targets were the Japanese carriers, including the *Zuikaku* and *Shokaku* which had fought the old USS *Lexington* in the Battle of the Coral Sea. Morever, *Zuikaku* was the last surviving Japanese aircraft carrier that participated in the Sunday morning sneak attack on Pearl Harbor. Mitscher had to take this chance to smash the Japanese carrier force.

Norman Sterrie led half of VT-16's aptly named TBM Avengers in pursuit of the retiring Japanese fleet. He recalls:
'The other half of our group with TBMs under command of Lt John Bowen was to follow, but, because their take-off time was getting later and later, the second half of the strike force was called off. We had a fix on the position of the Japanese forces, which by this time were mighty short of aircraft, except for defensive purposes. The day before they had lost a great part of their carrier-based air force. I assume, however, that considerable fighter protection was left for the force, as we discovered once we got to their position.

'Since I had been Executive Officer of VT-16 when Bob Isely was killed, I then took command of the squadron. Because our airplanes had radar, it was the torpedo squadron's responsibiity to lead the rest of the Air Group to the target. Our airplanes were also the slowest, so it was necessary for the other airplanes to throttle down to our speed in order to coordinate the attack. We knew that we were being launched toward a fleeing target, which would ordinarily be out of range. However, the planners calculated that they could proceed at full speed to get the carriers into position to recover all aircraft. If all went according to plan, we would not actually be out of range.

'As we approached the enemy fleet we were attacked by enemy fighters, which took all of our fighter cover away from us. During the last 10 or 15 miles to the target we were under fighter attack. During this period Lt Cushman's wingman, Warren McLellan, was shot down. The fighter attack was getting intense at that time and I observed that he went down in flames. We later learned that he and his crew were able to parachute out and that they had descended into the middle of the Japanese fleet. Fortunately, they were able to get into life rafts and, the next day, were picked up by rescue craft.

'It was quite apparent at this time that unless we pressed the attack very quickly, there wouldn't be anybody left to conduct it, since we were under heavy fighter attack. However, we were then picked up by anti-aircraft fire from the Japanese fleet and this event actually became our refuge. When we began to encounter ominous black puffs of smoke all around us, the Japanese fighters retreated, presumably to go after other targets.

'We each carried four 500lb semi-armour piercing (SAP) bombs. To coordinate the attack with the dive bombers, we formed a wide descending circle to the target, which was one of the carriers. The SBDs went straight down onto their objectives. We were not able to do that in our TBMs, so we had to begin a long descent, which was tracked by heavy AA fire. We managed to select the target carrier and then pushed our glide much faster than we would have liked. We went through heavy AA fire and dived our way through the rest of the Japanese fleet and out to relative safety.

'Once we got out of the Fleet disposition, the Japanese fighters picked us up again, but not for long. My gunner, AMM1c Jack Webb, shot one down, which was a great credit to him, for the need to defend ourselves in that manner was really quite limited. We generally could count upon complete protection from our own escorts.

'The return flight itself was a memorable one. It was getting late in the day and it was obvious as we started heading back that this was going to be a night carrier landing, involving hundreds of planes even though none of us had had any recent experience in night operations. There was no problem in locating our Task Force because Adm Mitscher had ordered all the ships' lights turned on to make their location very apparent.

'As we neared the fleet, however, it was very clear that there was much trouble ahead. We had truly struck out of range and now we had little fuel margin to allow for an orderly landing sequence. Consequently, the air waves were soon cluttered with all manner of instructions and requests. There was a note of panic in the voices of those pilots who were going down without being able to make a carrier landing at all.

'To make matters worse, there were accidents on the flight decks of several of the carriers. Planes were landing after being waved off, which was never heard of during the daytime – and shouldn't be at any time. Those landings only invited further crashes. The flight decks, therefore, were becoming quite cluttered and numbers of planes dared not even risk the last element of a carrier landing for fear of going down in a position less optimal than beside one of the destroyers.

'Since I was in the lead plane, I had no problem. I had made the most economical use of fuel, as I had not needed to jockey the throttle to hold any formation position. I circled above, waiting for the whole thing to quiet down. Meanwhile, I instructed my pilots to fend for themselves. Three of my planes went in, but all of the crews were rescued by the destroyers in the areas where they landed.

'After I landed aboard the *Lexington* I learned that of the six in our group, only Lt Kent Cushman and I had been able to make it back to our ship. That was certainly a depressing note to turn in on, but we were heartened the next day to learn that three of the crews had been picked up. Our joy was even greater when we received the news that Warran McLellan and his crew had also been rescued. Consequently, our losses for that operation were only the four TBMs that had

gone into the water. We regretted that we could not take off the following day and finish the job, but that was not the purpose of our total mission.'

The record shows that, even if the US Navy force had been able to continue the pursuit, there would have been little of the Japanese force left to attack. Indeed, that encounter was the last major use by the Japanese of carrier-based aircraft in the tradition of the Battles of the Coral Sea and Midway. The Japanese than had to make greater use of land-based aircraft as the Allies pressed closer to the home islands, thus giving the American carriers virtually unchallenged latitude to operate in the Philippine Sea, off Formosa and French Indo-China, and to interdict maritime traffic in Japan's closest sea lanes.

For Air Group 16 the fighting ended on 9 July 1944, when it was relieved in Kwajalein by Air Group 19. With the new Air Group aboard, USS *Lexington* returned to the war zone to face Kamikaze attacks and the final fury of the Japanese military effort.

Lt Norman Sterrie was assigned to staff duty with Fleet Air at NAS Alameda in California. Shortly after the war ended in 1945, he returned to his home in Minnesota and entered medical school to prepare himself for the profession he has pursued since then.

USS *Lexington*, which at this writing is the oldest aircraft carrier in the world still in active service, presently serves as the US Navy's training carrier and operates in the relatively calm waters of the Gulf of Mexico. She is slated to become a part of the US Naval Aviation Museum in Pensacola, Florida – demonstrating again the great survivability of the famed 'blue ghost of the Pacific'.

*Below:* Grumman F4F-4 Wildcats bearing neither rudder stripes nor red centres on stars./*US Navy*

# VB-3 at Midway

Bombing Squadron 3 was ashore at NAS North Island, near San Diego, California, when the Japanese attacked Pearl Harbor. The squadron's normal schedule called for it to deploy in a few days aboard USS *Saratoga*, which had just been overhauled at the Puget Sound, Washington naval shipyard. However, the events in Hawaii caused the schedule to be quickly moved up. While President Franklin D. Roosevelt was asking the US Congress for a formal declaration of war against the Japanese Empire the following day, 8 December 1941, VB-3 personnel were busily loading aboard *Saratoga*.

The carrier departed San Diego the next day and arrived at Pearl Harbor a week later to begin its – and VB-3's – first wartime cruise. The squadron's early operations are recalled by retired Rear-Adm Maxwell F. Leslie, a 1926 graduate of the US Naval Academy who had assumed command of VB-3 just before the new Douglas SBD-3 Dauntless dive bombers arrived in significant numbers during the summer of 1941. He remembers:

'Immediately upon leaving port my squadron and the scouting squadron, VS-3, commenced routine scouting missions from dawn to dusk, going out in two-plane sections as far as 250 miles. That was quite a feat because we had to rely principally on dead reckoning navigation to locate the carrier on our return, as radio silence was strictly enforced. This heavy schedule proved to be too much for our limited number of

18 aircraft per squadron and after a few days we had to resort to conducting missions with single aircraft that did not go out more than 150 miles.

'Before we went to the single-plane system, however, I almost lost my wingman, Lt Frank Bolles, who was also the squadron's Executive Officer. Frank and I were on the dusk patrol, which meant we were supposed to return to the *Saratoga* just before sunset. We were less than 100 miles from the ship when I happened to look back and see Frank's plane coming in low over the water and about to make a forced landing.

'I considered this event an emergency that justified breaking radio silence to report the incident and request assistance. But our ships were not equipped with radar and could not take bearings on me, so I had to circle the location of the downed aircraft until the nearest destroyer could reach the scene. Darkness was fast approaching and, with all of the ships in our formation under darkened ship conditions, it was apparent that I would have trouble finding the *Saratoga* upon my return.

'I was told by a member of the staff of Rear-Adm Aubrey F. Fitch, Commander of Task Force 14, to abandon my watch over the downed pilot and his radioman, but I requested to remain on station until the nearest destroyer arrived. It finally spotted the plane at about sunset and picked up the two-man crew. I then high-tailed it for the carrier at full throttle and arrived shortly after sundown.'

USS *Yorktown* repair crews at work following first attack during the Battle of Midway./*US Navy*

*Above:* USS *Yorktown* (CV-5) in drydock following damage sustained during the Battle of the Coral Sea./*US Navy*

Also aboard *Saratoga* during the first part of that cruise was the US Marine Corps fighter squadron VMF-221, which was being transported to Wake Island. When that bastion fell to Japanese forces, the Marine Grumman F4F-3 Wildcats went to Midway Island rather than Wake to participate in its defense. Meanwhile, *Saratoga* operated between Hawaii and Midway until 11 January 1942, when it was hit by an enemy torpedo. Admiral Leslie notes:

'This incident was unusual because, even though it took a direct hit, the carrier was able to increase speed and get out of the area. Upon returning from that operation, we were shore based in Hawaii for a few weeks and then we embarked aboard *Enterprise* with Adm W.F. Halsey and staff as part of Task Group 16.1 which accompanied *Hornet* (Task Group 16.2) when it launched Jimmy Doolittle's B-25 bomber force against Japan on 18 April.

'Aircraft from VB-3 were part of the advance scouting screen that encountered and fired on Japanese fishing or picket boats, some 600 miles off Japan, which we thought might sound the

first alarm that carriers were heading toward the country. Doolittle's planes were launched shortly thereafter and ahead of schedule because Adm Halsey didn't want his ships to be subjected to attack by shore-based aircraft or, for that matter, even to be discovered. We watched the Doolittle raiders take off from the *Hornet* and I remember wondering whether the first plane had enough speed to remain airborne after its short run off the carrier's flight deck.'

The success of the Doolittle attack silenced any remaining opposition to the eastward extension of the Japanese defence perimeter advocated by Japan's Commander-in-Chief of the Combined Fleet, Adm Isoroku Yamamoto. He proposed to establish a perimeter from the western Aleutian Islands to Midway, which would serve as a jumping off point for the subsequent invasion of Hawaii. In May Adm Yamamoto began Operation 'MI', sending one strike force that included a fleet carrier and a light carrier to the Aleutians while a much larger force set out for Midway. The latter force, commanded by Vice-

Adm Chuichi Nagumo, included four of the fleet carriers that had attacked Pearl Harbor, as well as a light carrier and other support ships.

VB-3, which had returned to Hawaii aboard *Enterprise* and then joined Task Force 17 aboard the hastily repaired *Yorktown*, was to play a key role in the forthcoming battle. Admiral Leslie recalls:

'When we departed Pearl Harbor during the latter part of May we were not informed about the prospective engagement. It was a very confidential subject, but we sensed that something big was brewing. During the passage from Pearl Harbor to the Midway area we learned that a large portion of the Japanese fleet was headed eastward toward an uncertain destination.

'A copy of my original report, written after the battle, begins with the words "Reports of the location of the subject Japanese carriers were received, in *Yorktown*, during the early morning

of 4 June." I believe these reports came from patrol aircraft operating from Midway.

'At the pre-launch conference Lt-Cdr John S. ("Jimmie") Thach, Commanding Officer of VF-3, advised that his F4F fighters would have a range of only about 175 miles if they were to have sufficient fuel for combat action and the return flight. Lt-Cdr Lance E. ("Lem") Massey, skipper of VT-3, had a flight of slow Douglas TBD Devastators that could do about 105kts and cover about the same 175-mile range. The SBDs used by VB-3 and VS-5 had a medium-range speed and probably the greatest range of all aircraft aboard *Yorktown*. Consequently, the first to be launched were VT-3's aircraft, armed with torpedoes and heading on a course that would intercept the Japanese carriers heading for Midway. Six of Jimmie Thach's fighters were then launched to accompany the torpedo planes, which were flying at a very low altitude of perhaps 500ft. It was a question whether Thach

*Below:* USS *Yorktown* (CV-5) at anchor prior to her wartime cruise./*US Navy*

*Bottom:* Officers of VB-3 pose aboard USS *Yorktown* (CV-5) on 5 December 1941, two days before the US was attacked by Japan and entered World War 2. Front row (left to right): Loring Siegner, Osborne Wiseman, 'Bones' Savage, Dave Shumway, Max Leslie, Franke Bolles, Ralph Arent, Syd Bottomley and Jim Ready. Back row: Paul Schlegel, Roy Isaman, 'Soupy' Campbell. George Friend, A. W. Hanson, Bob Elder, Gordon Sherwood, Charlie Lane and Paul Norby. /*Rear-Adm M. F. Leslie*

would escort VT-3 or VB-3. I suggested they accompany VT-3 and Massey said he thought they should go with VB-3. Thach said, "I think I should go with the torpedo planes" and we all agreed. He only had six planes so he could only cover one squadron. Unfortunately he couldn't save VT-3 but on the other hand no Jap fighters attacked VB-3 so he made the best of a tragic situation. The balance of his planes remained with the ship for Combat Air Patrol.

'The position report received at 0645 that day placed the Japanese carriers 156 miles northwest of Midway. It was assumed aboard the *Yorktown* that the Japanese would proceed at about 25kts on a line toward Midway from that position. This direction was also into the surface wind, which was approximately 15 to 20kts from the southeast. That would be their probable heading for launching or recovering aircraft.

'Therefore, 17 SBDs from my squadron, were launched beginning at 1045 with orders to intercept the Japanese using their last known position, 156 miles northwest of Midway, and assuming they were heading for the island at 25kts. We were to turn north if they were not sighted when their proposed track had been reached. The squadron departed in three divisions at 1102 on a track of 225 to 230 degrees at a ground speed of about 120mph. Aircraft and crews were as follows:

**First Division**

3-B-1 Lt-Cdr M.F. Leslie, ARMlc W.E. Gallagher

3-B-2 Lt(jg) P.A. Holmberg, AMM2c G.A. La Plant

3-B-3 Ens P.W. Schlegel, ARM2c J.A. Shropshire

3-B-4 Ens R.K. Campbell, AMMlc H.H. Craig

3-B-5 Ens A.W. Hanson, ARM3c J.J. Godfrey

3-B-6 Ens R.H. Benson, ARM3c F.P. Bergeron

## Second Division

3-B-7 Lt(jg) G.A. Sherwood, ARM2c H.D. Bennett

3-B-8 Ens R.M. Isaman, ARM3c S.K. Weaver

3-B-9 Ens P.W. Cobb, AMM2c C.E. Zimmerman

3-B-10 Lt H.S. Bottomley, Jr, AMM2c D.F. Johnson

3-B-11 Ens C.S. Lane, ARM2c J.L. Henning

3-B-12 Ens J.C. Butler, ARM3c D.D. Berg

## Third Division

3-B-13 Lt D.W. Shumway, ARM1c R.E. Coons

3-B-14 Ens R.M. Elder, RM3c L.A. Till

3-B-15 Ens B.R. Cooner, AOM2c C.R. Bassett

3-B-16 Lt(jg) O.B. Wiseman, ARM3c G.U. Dawn

3-B-17 Ens M.A. Merrill, RM3c D.J. Bergeron

'After leaving the ship and joining VT-3 and VF-3, we climbed to 15,000ft to use possible cloud cover, but the weather was clear, to screen our approach and give us greater visibility and of course be at the proper altitude to attack. Due to a faulty bomb release connection, however, my airplane and three others – 3-B-8, 3-B-11 and 3-B-17 – inadvertently dropped their 1,000lb bombs soon after departure. Just prior to this engagement, new electrical bomb release mechanisms had been installed in our aircraft to replace manually-operated systems that did not

possess an instantaneous release feature. The new mechanisms were set on "safe" prior to take-off and we believe they released the bombs when they were set on "armed" once we were in flight. In any event, we proceeded to the target minus four of our most effective weapons. My personal dilemma was great because of losing my bomb. Returning for another one was definitely ruled out. I decided to continue so as to retain command, make a good dive thus giving the squadron a good start and shoot my .50 cal fixed guns. It developed that everything worked out well for VB-3.

'Once over the target I knew we could depend on our SBDs to do a really superb job. The Dauntless had many fine features: it was steady in a dive, could carry a 1,000lb bomb, had good range, two well-placed .50 cal fixed machine guns, a twin mount .30 cal flexible weapon for the radioman/rear gunner, excellent radio and homing equipment, armour behind the pilot's back and for the rear gunner, automatic flight control that was most welcome on long flights and scouting missions, leak proof fuel tanks, good speed, and the power you needed to reach altitude.

'The one bad feature of the SBD, which you couldn't blame on the airplane, was the bomb sight. It usually fogged over during a dive because of the rapidly changing atmospheric conditions. This fault made it necessary at times for pilots to use an open sight, which cut down on

*Top:* Japanese aircraft carrier IJNS *Akagi./US Navy*

*Above:* Another view of the Japanese aircraft carrier IJNS *Akagi./US Navy*

accuracy. The skill displayed by our dive bomber pilots in battle was outstanding because it was most difficult to hit a moving target, such as a ship zigzagging at 25kts. I think that feat can be compared to dropping a marble from eye height on a fast moving cockroach.

'At 1145 my squadron was at 15,000ft and we passed directly over VT-3's 11 TBDs accompanied by Jimmie Thach's six F4F-3s. Upon reaching the projected line of the enemy carriers possibly headed for Midway and not sighting them, at 1200 Lem Massey changed his course to a northwest heading of about 345 degrees and we followed them. In spite of strict radio silence, I sent a coded message to Massey, as well as to his Executive Officer, Lt P.H. Hart, asking if they had sighted the Japanese. There was no reply.

'Then at about 1205 my radioman, Gallagher, pointed out the wakes of ships some 35 to 40 miles dead ahead. At about this time the air became filled with radio messages and it was evident that VT-3 was being attacked by Japanese fighter aircraft.

'Those fighters were undoubtedly stationed there to intercept any aircraft that might have come from Midway. Indeed, some of the Zeros had belly tanks, which further indicates they were on patrol. They dropped their tanks when they encountered VT-3 and Jimmie Thach's six fighters. I'm really not sure why the Zeros were at low altitude instead of being high, but it is possible the Japanese didn't have enough aircraft to cover both areas.

'At the time they were attacked, the VT-3 aircraft were flying at about 500ft so as to stay beneath radar, if the Japanese had it. Also, the torpedo aircraft had to be low to attack and they could better protect themselves at low altitude. But the altitude didn't help. I subsequently learned that Lem Massey's was probably the first VT-3 airplane shot down and he went down in flames. There were only two or three survivors from the entire squadron of 11 planes.

'There is no telling what would have happened if the Zeros had been at high altitude because VB-3 had no fighter protection and we were at 20,000ft, where the Zeros were most effective. As it turned out, my squadron encountered no enemy fighters, which was fortunate. It again indicated the possibility that the Japanese ships didn't have radar, which could have detected us so fighters could have been vectored to intercept us.

'Very soon thereafter it became apparent that a major portion of the Japanese attack force was in sight. All ships – probably a total of 12, including three and possibly four carriers – were zigzagging and going at high speed. In view of the intense opposition by Japanese Zeros attacking VT-3 and possibly other complications, I was unable to establish radio communication with Lt-Cdr Massey or anyone else except within my own squadron. Accordingly, I had no choice but to abandon the plan for a coordinated attack. It was planned for VB-3 to attack first followed by VT-3 which ideally would approach the target

coming from various directions thus making hits regardless of which direction the target turned. Next the fighters would strafe the target if not required for protection of VT-3 (or VB-3).

'SBDs from VS-5, commanded by Lt W.C. Short, were scheduled to take off from the *Yorktown* after VB-3 and proceed as a second wave, arriving at the target shortly after the other *Yorktown* squadrons. Consequently, at about 1215, I sent a radio message to Lt Short and ordered him to attack the smaller carrier next to the big one I had selected for VB-3. Some of our pilots reported it was really a big one of the "Essex" class, which is 26,000 tons. One pilot said, ". . . it was the biggest damn thing he had ever seen." I later learned, however, that VS-5 had not taken off. It had remained aboard the carrier for follow-up action.

'We began descending to pick up speed and at 1223 my radioman reported that the carrier I had chosen for target was launching aircraft. We had strict orders to maintain radio silence or at least, in an emergency, to talk in code. But now everything began to happen so fast that there was no time to look up the proper code words, write them down, broadcast the message and at the same time fly the aircraft and keep track of all the other events that were going on. So we did the best we could.

'I again tried to contact Lt-Cdr Massey or Lt Hart in plain language, but without success. I thought it was vital for a coordinated attack. Feeling I had done all I could to attack as planned, without further delay I gave my squadron the signal to attack. At about 1225 I led the squadron in a dive from 14,500ft. We came down with the sun at our backs, on a course from southeast to northwest. Our target was a large carrier with a full-length flight deck that had a big red rising sun – or "meatball" – in the centre. The general characteristics of the ship fit the description we had of the *Kaga*.

'Although my 1,000lb bomb had dropped prematurely, I had to lead the squadron in the dive, as the initial dive made in a formation attack is the most important. When we got down to about 10,000ft, I drew a bead on the target by firing my two .50 cal fixed machine guns at the superstructure, which was on the starboard side one third way aft from the bow. I did not receive AA fire. My bullets appeared to be hitting the bridge. When I got down to bomb release altitude both guns suddenly jammed and, in spite of my frantic efforts, they wouldn't recharge.

'After levelling off from my attack I looked back just in time to see the second plane, piloted by Lt(jg) Paul ("Lefty") Holmberg, drop his bomb which made a direct hit on the flight deck. It was the first bomb dropped in the battle. The bomb exploded in the midst of a pack of aircraft spotted just aft of the superstructure. The explosion turned the after part of the flight deck into sheets of flame and blew an airplane over the side just as it was being launched. Holmberg's plane received heavy anti-aircraft fire, which he passed through.

'Seconds later there was another terrific explosion on deck. Next came a near miss on the starboard bow. The carrier was then practically engulfed in flames and black smoke, which made the point of aim more difficult for the pilots who followed. However, in quick succession – spaced to allow for a proper dive interval – I next observed three or four separate explosions similar to the initial one. The flames, various-coloured debris, smoke and steam that we could see indicated that the interior of the ship must have been an inferno beyond belief.

'As I retired from the scene at about 50ft altitude, the water around my plane was sprinkled with shrapnel from the destroyers escorting the blazing carrier, but there were no hits.

'I then circled the designated squadron rendezvous area, but only the plane piloted by Ens Hanson joined me. When I began circling I could see the entire Japanese formation and none of the other ships appeared to be in distress. At about 1228 however, there were three to five huge explosions in quick succession, followed by flames and smoke on each of two ships that we thought were carriers located 10 to 12 miles west of our target. I believe that either or both of these explosions were caused by the *Enterprise* and *Hornet* air groups.

'Ens Hanson and I departed for the *Yorktown*

*Above:* Douglas TBD-1s of VT-6 and Grumman F4F-3s of VF-6 are spotted on the flight deck of USS *Enterprise* (CV-6) while accompanying USS *Hornet* (CV-8) during the launch of the Doolittle raiders in 1942./*US Navy*

at 1242. We were joined enroute by 10 more VB-3 planes, which had hit the Japanese carrier and other targets. Ens R.M. (Bob) Elder and Ens B.R. (Randy) Cooner were the last pilots to dive and seeing the target was obviously out of action, they wisely diverted their attention to a light cruiser. They scored a hit on the fantail and a near miss. LT(jg) Osborn B. Wiseman and Ens John C. Butler made a similar observation and attacked a nearby battleship, scoring a direct hit on the stern and a near miss. As accurately as I have learned a recap of bombs dropped from our 17 planes is as follows:

4 dropped prematurely
2 dropped on light cruisers scoring 1 hit 1 near miss
2 dropped on battleship scoring 1 hit 1 near miss
3-5 dropped on carrier hits
4 dropped on carrier near misses

This is considered to be an outstanding performance.

'Eventually all 17 of VB-3's aircraft rendezvoused and, thanks to our recently installed radio direction finders, we got back over the *Yorktown* about 1320 and circled the ship. We were ready to begin landing at 1345 when the ship signalled via radio for us to form a Combat Air Patrol because another enemy attack was imminent.

'The ship had repelled one attack but had sustained serious damage. Just prior to the second attack the *Yorktown* was able to get up enough speed for Jimmie Thach and several of his VF-3 fighters to land aboard. In view of the impending attack, however, the carrier's gasoline system had been purged as a normal fire prevention procedure and that meant his fighters could not be refuelled. The *Yorktown* was practically dead in the water at this point, but eventually worked up enough speed to launch several VF-3 planes. The decision to launch fighters was prompted by Jimmie telling the ship's commanding officer, Capt Elliott Buckmaster, that he wished every plane with at least 30 gallons of fuel to take off. They did launch a number before the second attack began. Jimmie and his fighters shot down several Japanese planes, as did the ship's anti-aircraft guns. But nothing could stop the Japanese from eventually sending at least two torpedoes into the port side of *Yorktown*.

'Our section was useless as a CAP. My machine guns were irreparably jammed and my wingman, Lt(jg) Holmberg, advised me that his wheels would not retract; they had been lowered in preparation for landing aboard *Yorktown* and now it seemed that a bullet hole in his hydraulic system made his landing gear inoperable. Hence, we were ordered by the ship to stay clear of the anti-aircraft fire and to try to make it to Task Force 16, which was then in sight.

'At about this time, however, my radioman, Gallagher, said he sighted a rubber boat in the water some eight to ten miles from *Yorktown*. A closer inspection revealed that "the boat" was a

TBD supported by two flotation bags. Two survivors were on the wings, which were awash. I then wrote a message, which I dropped in a sandbag on the forecastle of the nearest destroyer, USS *Hammann* (DD-412).* That ship was already en route to pick up two men from VS-6 so I had to go back and locate "my" pilot and use a signal light to direct the destroyer to his location. The downed pilot was W.G. Esders, who was then an enlisted Chief Aviation Pilot attached to VT-3. As far as I know, he was the only survivor of the ill-fated flight of VT-3. His radioman, Robert B. Braziers, was wounded and died soon after he was rescued.

'I then returned with my wingman to the *Yorktown* and attempted to get the bearing and distance to Task Force 16. The ship had been heavily bombed and I don't think their radio equipment was functioning properly; moreover, there were serious problems aboard ship, coping with damage from the attack.

'When I finally received the information I needed, I was so low on gasoline that I could not

*This ship was named in honour of Ens Charles H. Hammann, the second US Navy pilot to be awarded the Medal of Honour. Ensign Hammann was one of a group of American naval aviators attached to the 263a Squadriglia Macchi of the Royal Italian Air Force, stationed at Porto Corsino, Italy. On 21 August 1918 he landed his Macchi seaplane on the water within five miles of the Austrian naval base at Pola and succeeded in rescuing a downed squadronmate, Ens George M. Ludlow.

have gotten aboard a Task Force 16 carrier unless they could have taken me immediately. In the meantime, my wingman told me that he had even less gasoline than I, due to the fact that he had been flying with his landing gear extended. That fact and the lack of knowledge about the status of Task Force 16 prompted me to tell Holmberg that both of us would have to make water landings in the vicinity of the *Yorktown*.

'We decide to land alongside the heavy cruiser *Astoria* (CA-34), which was dead in the water while awaiting transfer from the *Yorktown* of Rear-Adm Frank J. Fletcher and his staff. Our landing was timed just right because the transfer of the staff had been completed and, unbeknown to us another attack on the *Yorktown* was imminent, thus making it necessary for the *Astoria* to get underway, which it did instantly after we got aboard. In another minute the ship would have abandoned us, so we were told.

'We made our landing at 1610 after having been in the air for five hours and 27 minutes. A normal SBD flight would have had us back to the carrier in about four hours. About five minutes later, the next attack on *Yorktown* began and all I could do was watch it from the quarterdeck of the *Astoria*. Japanese torpedo planes penetrated the most intense anti-aircraft fire I ever witnessed. It was an unbelievably courageous performance by the Japanese pilots that I did not see matched until the Kamikaze attacks later in the war. On this occasion, however, two or three torpedo planes were at about 150ft altitude and

*Below:* USS *Yorktown* under attack./*US Navy*

came within 600yd of *Yorktown* before dropping their torpedoes. I saw the torpedoes in the air, as they left the airplanes, and then there were two hits on the port quarter. The planes were downed almost immediately after they dropped.

'It should be noted that prior to Midway the *Yorktown* had received a hurried repair job at Pearl Harbor necessitated by previous bomb damage during the Coral Sea battle and that Capt Buckmaster wasn't convinced that the ship's watertight integrity was up to par. Hence, following the torpedo hits the ship took a list which went to 26 degrees. Counter flooding wasn't possible because of the loss of power and the captain feared that *Yorktown* would roll over with a horrible loss of over 2,000 men. Therefore his only choice was to abandon ship.

'Thanks to efficient organization by Capt Buckmaster, good weather and available rescue ships, the action was carried out with no loss of life except those who died during the attacks. Capt Buckmaster made a final inspection of the ship, found nothing to change his decision and then slid down a line over the stern and into the water, being the last man to leave the ship. Just before leaving the ship Capt Buckmaster's Orderly offered to give him his life preserver but, of course, it was refused. Capt Buckmaster then relieved his Orderly from duty so he could abandon the ship. Capt Buckmaster found a life preserver when he got into the water and then, seeing a Ward Room mess attendant who couldn't swim slide off a life raft, Capt Buckmaster pulled the man back to the raft. (Some years later the man, then a mailman showed up delivering the mail to Capt Buckmaster's Coronada home.) Buckmaster was picked up by the destroyer *Hammann* and then transferred to the *Astoria*.

'It was a sobering, impressive, sorrowful yet rewarding sight to see this gallant officer plod his way up the gangway of the *Astoria*. He was wearing a khaki uniform, hatless and coatless in an open-neck shirt. He was ringing wet from perspiration and salt water, and had absolutely nothing in his possession except an indomitable

spirit to continue the action, God willing. He gained a brief respite before gathering a crew of volunteers to accompany him back to the *Yorktown* the next day to attempt to save the ship.

'He and about 170 selected volunteer officers and men were returned via the *Hammann* to the *Yorktown*, where they arrived before dawn on 6 June. With the *Hammann* secured alongside, they boarded the carrier and commenced the Herculean task of trying to save the *Yorktown* and have it towed back to Hawaii at a speed of three to four knots.

'However, fate decreed the *Yorktown*'s doom. In spite of normal precautionary measures, such as anti-submarine patrols by our destroyers, an enemy submarine penetrated the defense and at about 1330 fired four torpedoes at close range. The *Hammann* was hit, broke in two and sank in about four minutes with heavy loss of life. *Yorktown* received another underwater blow that made the task of Capt Buckmaster and his volunteers insurmountable. They were transferred to the destroyer USS *Benham* (DD-397), from where they could keep a close watch on the *Yorktown* in hopes of resuming the salvage operation at first light the next morning.

'Capt Buckmaster's plans were again thwarted because during the night the *Yorktown* suddenly increased itys list and at 0600 on 7 June, it rolled over and sank with a horrible rattle of loose gear. All attendant ships half-masted their colours and all hands uncovered and came to attention.'

Due to the hectic series of events, Rear-Adm (then Lt-Cdr) Leslie did not return to VB-3. Initially he was listed as missing in action; hence, command of the squadron passed to his Executive Officer, Lt DeWitt W. ('Dave') Shumway who had landed aboard *Enterprise* with all VB-3 planes except Leslie's and Holmberg's.

Further events of VB-3's actions during the Battle of Midway are contained in Lt Shumway's report, written as a third-person narrative identifying both men and aircraft involved in

*Below:* Douglas TBD-1s of VT-6 are readied for take-off during the Battle of Midway. Only four VT-6 aircraft returned./*US Navy*

what proved to be the destruction by US carrier planes of four of the six fleet carriers that had participated in the sneak attack on Pearl Harbor.

His report picks up the story of the attack after VB-3 regrouped aboard *Enterprise*:

'First day, 4 June. Second phase: At 1730 VB-3, now composed of 14 SBDs, was launched from the *Enterprise* in company with six VS-6 planes and four VB-6 planes as a result of a new contact with the enemy fleet by VS-5 scout planes. The enemy was reported to consist of one carrier, two battleships, three heavy cruisers, and four destroyers. The attack group was under the command of Commander VS-6 (Lt Wilmer E. Gallaher). VB-3's tactical organisation was as follows:

3-B-13 Lt D.W. Shumway, ARM1c R.E. Coons
3-B-15 Ens B.R. Cooner, AOM2c C.R. Bassett
3-B-3 Ens P.W. Schlegel, ARM2c J.A. Shropshire

3-B-16 Lt(jg) O.B. Wiseman, ARM3c G.U. Dawn
3-B-17 Ens M.A. Merrill, RM3c D.J. Bergeron

6-B-12 Ens S.C. Hogan, Jr (VB-6), S/1c E.K. Braun

3-B-7 Lt (jg) G.A. Sherwood, ARM2c H.D. Bennett
3-B-8 Ens R.M. Isaman, ARM3c S.K. Weaver
3-B-9 Ens P.W. Cobb, AMM2c C.E. Zimmerman

3-B-10 Lt H.S. Bottomley, Jr, AMM2c D.F. Johnson
3-B-11 Ens C.S. Lane, ARM2c J.L. Henning
3-B-12 Ens J.C. Butler, ARM3c D.D. Berg

3-B-4 Ens R.K. Campbell, AMM1c H.H. Craig
3-B-5 Ens A.W. Hanson, ARM3c J.J. Godfrey
3-B-6 Ens R.H. Benson, ARM3c F.P. Bergeron

This is the same organisation as the first phase except for 6-B-12 and less Lt-Cdr Leslie and Lt(jg) Holmberg.

'At 1750 the group took departure from Task Force 16 and commenced climbing for attack position. The enemy was first sighted to the northwest about 30 miles distant at 1845 from 13,00ft on a westerly course, speed 20kts. Their formation was again widely spaced, as in the previous attack, with little or no screening. The air group immediately swung wide to the southwest in order to approach from the direction of the sun. Weather conditions were ideal with excellent visibility, unlimited ceiling, low scattered clouds at 2,500ft and smooth sea.

'By 1858 the group was in attack position, altitude 19,000ft, approaching the enemy at high speed from the sun; divisions and sections were stacked down. Commander VS-6 directed by voice radio the *Enterprise* planes to attack the lone carrier, believed to be of the "Hoyso" [sic] class,* and VB-3 to attack the nearer battleship. At the same time it was announced that enemy fighters were ahead and above. These were

*This is a misspelling, as there was no 'Hoyso' class of Japanese aircraft carriers. Lt Shumway probably meant to refer to the fleet carrier *Hiryu*, which was close enough in appearance to the *Soryu* to lead to the conclusion that the two ships were of the same class.

*Below:* Heavy listing sets in after USS *Yorktown* is torpedoed. /US Navy

*Bottom:* Ordnancemen of VS-6 load 500lb bomb beneath a Douglas SBD aboard USS *Enterprise* (CV-6) during raids on Guadalcanal and Tulagi on 7 August 1942./US Navy

*Above:* Japanese aircraft carrier IJNS *Hiryu* burning after being attacked by VB-3 during the Battle of Midway./*US Navy*

carriers out of action. This one the *Hiryu* and *Kaga* during the morning attack.

'Retirement was effected by radically manoeuvring at high speed near the water both to the east and southwest through heavy anti-aircraft fire and fighter attacks.

'3-B-13, Lt Shumway, was attacked by three fighters, both during the dive and retirement, which made sweeping passes from the rear. Two of these were lost in clouds, the other continuing the attack during retirement in the clouds, firing small-calibre sighting shots wth intermittent 20mm cannon. The plane was hit by several 20mm shells, damaging right diving and landing flap, right main gas tank (resulting in loss of all fuel remaining in that tank), right elevator and stabilizer, and baggage compartment, exploding therein and throwing fragments into the rear cockpit, which resulted in injuring the gunner, ARMlc R.E. Coons, slightly in the left arm. Several small-calibre holes were later discovered about the fuselage and nose section.

'3-B-15, Ens B.R. Cooner, was similarly attacked by three fighters which used the same tactics. The pilot also believes some of the fighters to have been Me-109s.* One 20-mm shell passed through the rear cockpit, exploding in the radio transmitter, thereby seriously wounding the gunner, AOM2c C.R. Bassett. The pilot received a slight leg wound. One explosive small calibre bullet entered and shattered the life raft compartment. One Zero fighter was shot down by twin mount .30 cal fire, according to the gunner.

'Likewise, Ens M.A. Merrill, pilot of 3-B-17, was attacked by two enemy fighters which used scissor tactics, diving simultaneously from high on each quarter. These broke off the attack after about five minutes, damaging the fuselage with small calibrfe fire. Two 20-mm shells struck just aft of the rear cockpit, fraying control cables slightly and injuring the gunner, RM3c D.J. Bergeron, in both feet.

'3-B-7, Lt(jg) G.A. Sherwood, had an experience similar to Ens Merrill's in 3-B-17, but sustained no damage.

'3-B-10, Lt H.S. Bottomley, was attacked at the top of his dive by a single fighter which made an overhead pass. He opened his diving flaps, thereby causing the enemy pilot to overshoot. Meanwhile, two other fighters attacked from overhead, rear, but their runs were spoiled by the first fighter, who pulled up vertically into them. At about 7,000ft in the dive another fighter appeared and commenced runs, which from a vertical attitude, appeared to be a form of "falling leaf". This plane was driven off by twin flexible .30 cal fire shortly thereafter. No damage was sustained.

believed to consist of at least 12 of the Zero type. At 1905 amidst heavy anti-aircraft fire, VS-6 broke off to commence the attack. While these planes were in the dive, the enemy carrier swung sharply to a southerly heading. Observing no direct hits by the VS-6 planes, VB-3 changed the objective from the battleship to the carrier, which was the primary objective ordered, and commenced the attack. [Rear-Adm Leslie considers the tactical decision, at the target, by Lt Shumway to attack the undamaged carrier, in lieu of his orders to attack the battleship, to have displayed outstanding judgement worthy of commendation. The carrier was the *Hiryu* which had launched planes for the *coup de grace* on the *Yorktown*. VB-6 dived last.] 3-B-13, 3-B-15, 3-B-10 and 3-B-17 (Shumway, Cooner, Bottomley and Merrill) were attacked in a dive by the enemy fighters. 3-B-12 and 3-B-16 (Butler and Wiseman) were reported to have been attacked by fighters and are believed to have been shot down. It is further believed that these casualties occurred after releasing their bombs. 3-B-4 and 3-B-6 (Campbell and Benson) attacked the battleship as previously directed, scoring a near miss and a direct hit which started fires. There were four direct hits by VB-3 alone on the carier and it was burning furiously. Thus VB-3 attacked and single handedly put two of the four enemy

*There was no navalised version of the Messerschmitt Bf109; hence, this misidentification is probably due to the swirl of events. At this time Japanese fleet carriers deployed with the Mitsubishi A6M2 Navy Type 0 Carrier Fighter Model 21, which was code-named 'Zeke', but generally referred to as 'Zero'.

*Above:* Flight deck crews prepare aircraft to take off from USS *Enterprise* (CV-6) during the Battle of Santa Cruz in October 1942./*US Navy*

'The squadron returned to the *Enterprise* between 2008 and 2034, landing aboard. Two planes failed to return: 3-B-12, Ens J.C. Butler, pilot, and ARM3c D.D. Berg, passenger; and 3-B-16, Lt(jg) O.B. Wiseman, pilot, and ARM3c G.U. Dawn, passenger.

'The damage sustained by 3-B-13, 3-B-15 and 3-B-17 rendered them inoperative for further combat.

'Second day, 5 June: At 1740, VB-3 was launched from the *Enterprise* in company with VB-6, VS-6 and VS-5 to attack and sink a crippled enemy carrier. The estimated location of the enemy force was 250 miles west northwest.

'The flight remained at a low altitude until approximately 100 miles from the anticipated enemy position. VS squadrons were on a scouting line. At this point the VB squadrons started climbing to altitude. At 2000 the position at which the enemy was expected to be was reached. The ceiling was 13,000ft, above which was a heavy overcast; visibility conditions were hazy. There was no appreciable amount of wind and the sea was smooth.

'As the enemy was nowhere in sight, the next 20 minutes were spent searching to the southwest. At 2020 a lone enemy vessel was sighted, believed to be a light cruiser of the *Katori* class, on course west, speed 25kts. It was

decided to attack this light cruiser, as it was growing dark, remaining gasoline load prevented further search, and there were no more enemy ships in the vicinity.

'The attack was initiated by VB-3 from an altitude of 13,000ft followed in order by VB-6, VS-6 and VS-5. Because of the cruiser's high speed, manoeuvrability, and the hazy weather conditions, a very elusive dive bombing target was presented. The enemy threw up a large volume of small-calibre intermittent anti-aircraft fire. There were no direct hits observed.

'The squadron made a running rendezvous and then proceeded back to the *Enterprise*, arriving over the ship at 2145 and landing aboard during darkness. All VB-3 planes returned undamaged. It was an outstanding performance to go out 250 miles and have all planes return to the carrier during darkness – night flying was difficult because pilots did not have the training or instruments for such flights.

'Third day, 6 June: Ten SBDs of VB-3 were ordered to proceed to the vicinity of Lat. 29-33 N, Long. 175-36 E, and attack a force reported to consist of a battleship and four destroyers. Five planes of VB-6 formed a third division and 16 planes of VS-5 and VS-6 combined to form another squadron. Twelve F4F-4s of VF-6 were launched to strafe the enemy destroyers, and

*Top:* Lt Walter L. Chewning, Catapult Officer aboard USS *Enterprise* (CV-6), scrambles up the side of an F6F that rolled into the port catwalk after landing. He saved the Hellcat pilot, Ens Byron M. Johnson, before the aircraft was completely enveloped in flames./*US Navy*

*Above:* Douglas SBD Dauntless aircraft flying over burning Japanese ship during the Battle of Midway./*US Navy*

three TBDs of VT-6 completed the group, which was under the command of Commander VS-5 [Lt Wallace C. Short, whose unit (designated VB-5 prior to the Battle of Midway) was initially aboard *Yorktown* along with VB-3].

'At 1240 the group was launched from the *Enterprise* and at 1300 took departure and proceeded on a southwesterly heading in the direction of the enemy contact. On the way the group climbed to 15,000ft and made contact at about 1400 with an enemy force to the southwest, distance 30 miles, consisting of one battle or heavy cruiser of the "Mogami" class,

one heavy cruiser believed to be of the "Atago" class, and two destroyers, course southwest, speed 15kts. Visibility was excellent, ceiling unlimited with low scattered clouds, wind 18kts from the southwest.

'As this force apparently did not contain a battleship, which was the specific objective, the group swung south around this force for 30 mile, endeavouring to locate the battleship to no avail. At length the Commander of VS-5 gave orders to attack the "Mogami" class cruiser, or battle cruiser as the case may be, at 1445. Divisions and sections made individual approaches from all directions. The attacks commenced at 1450 with little anti-aircraft fire encountered. There was no enemy air opposition.

'Individual VB-3 hits on the "Mogami" type are believed to be four direct hits and five near misses. After the attacks had been completed, the topside was burning heavily; the ship, a complete shambles, slowed to a stop. Many topside personnel had either been blown or jumped into the water. Internal explosions were seen to follow.

'3-B-8, Ens R.K. Isaman, dove on an "Atago" class heavy cruiser upon seeing it undamaged, and, through heavy anti-aircraft fire directed at him alone, scored a direct hit aft. Another direct hit followed soon thereafter on this ship. No heavy fires were started, however, although its speed was undoubtedly reduced.

'The F4F-4s made one pass at the destroyers, strafing them and then retiring.

'The TBDs had orders not to go into anti-aircraft fire and therefore retired without launching torpedoes.

'All ten planes of VB-3 returned undamaged and landed aboard the *Enterprise* at 1545.'

BOMBING SQUADRON THREE          SEPT.

The US Navy was the clear winner of the Battle of Midway. True, it had lost the aircraft carrier *Yorktown*, but its aircraft sunk four Japanese fleet aircraft carriers: *Kaga*, *Akagi*, *Hiryu* and *Soryu*. The battlecruiser *Mogami* was so badly damaged that it took two years to make all the repairs necessary to make her seaworthy again. The cruiser *Mikuma* was sunk with some 1,000 officers and men aboard her.

Turning back the Japanese at Midway is generally regarded as the turning point in the war in the Pacific. VB-3's significant role in that action was recognised by the US government, which bestowed a large number of its highest military awards on members of the 'Panther' squadron.

Lt-Cdr Maxwell F. Leslie was awarded the Navy Cross, as was his wingman, Lt(jg) Paul A. Holmberg. Leslie's executive officer, Lt DeWitt W. Shumway also received the Navy Cross, as did seven other VB-3 pilots: Ens Robert H. Benson, Ens Philip W. Cobb, Lt Harold S. Bottomley, Jr, Ens John C. Butler, Ens Robert M. Elder, Ens Bunyan R. Cooner, and Lt(jg) Osborne B. Wiseman.

Six backseatmen were awarded the Distinguished Flying Cross: AMMlc Horace H. Craig, ARM2c Jack C. Henning, ARM3c David D. Berg, ARMlc Ray E. Coons, ARM3c Leslie A. Till, AOM2c Clifton R. Bassett, Jr, and ARM3c G.U. Dawn.

VB-3's two pilot casualties, Ens John C. Butler and Lt(jg) Osborne B. Wiseman, were commemorated by destroyer escorts named in their honour: USS *Butler* (DE-339) and USS *Wiseman* (DE-667).

The squadron's first wartime skipper, Lt-Cdr Maxwell F. Leslie, was promoted to the rank of

*Above:* VB-3 aircrewmen pose before the 'island' superstructure of USS *Saratoga* (CV-3), their next carrier assignment after USS *Yorktown* (CV-5) was sunk during the Battle of Midway.
/*Capt H. S. Bottomley via R. L. Lawson*

*Left:* Among the several recipients of the Navy Cross in VB-3 was Lt H. S. Bottomley, Jr, seen here being decorated by Adm W. F. Halsey on 26 September 1942.
/*Capt H. S. Bottomley via R. L. Lawson*

Commander right after the Battle of Midway and became Commander of the Air Group (CAG) aboard USS *Enterprise*. He later enjoyed a fruitful naval career culminating in his promotion to Flag rank.

As for VB-3, the squadron went on to other battles, operating from other US Navy aircraft carriers, including the second USS *Yorktown* (CV-10), and continued to build its combat record on its great victory at the Battle of Midway.

# Red Rippers Over Casablanca

The wide scope of operations in the Pacific Theatre required a heavy commitment of US Navy aircraft carriers in that area. Most of the CVs, all of the CVLs and the majority of the CVEs were deployed to fight the Japanese. Thus, operations involving large carriers in the Atlantic and the Mediterranean were undertaken primarily by the Royal Navy.

By the autumn of 1942, however, the timing was right for Anglo-American carrier operations in support of a major objective. Events in the Pacific had stabilised enough for the United States to join with Britain in the invasion of Vichy French territory in North Africa. Operation 'Torch', as it was called, comprised three elements: a Western Naval Task Force

from the United States to take Casablanca on the Atlantic coast and Central and Eastern Task Forces from Britain to invade Oran and Algiers, respectively. The Royal Navy fleet carriers HMS *Formidable*, *Victorious*, *Furious* and *Argus* were joined by the escort carriers HMS *Biter*, *Dasher* and *Avenger*. The American element, Task Force 34, had air support from the fleet carrier USS *Ranger* (CV-4) and the escort carriers USS *Sangamon* (ACV-26), *Suwannee* (ACV-27), *Chenango* (ACV-28) and *Santee* (ACV-29).

USS *Ranger* was the smallest of the American fleet carriers. It was 769ft long and displaced 14,500ton. Yet, for this operation *Ranger* was able to deploy with an impressive number of aircraft: two fighter squadrons, VF-9 and VF-41, each equipped with 27 Grummman F4F-4

Wildcats, and the scouting squadron VS-41, equipped with 18 Douglas SBD-3 Dauntlesses.

Maynard M. ('Bud') Furney, now an aerospace engineer, was a member of VF-41, better known as the 'Red Rippers' and heir to one of the oldest fighter squadron traditions in the US Navy. Furney was an Ensign when he joined the squadron in January 1940 and began his service career flying Grumman F3F biplane fighters. As he points out, he quickly learned the Red Rippers' history and traditions, beginning with VF-41's distinctive squadron insignia:
'I was told that this piece of military heraldry was designed during a Friday afternoon conclave at the "Men Only" bar in the Officers' Club at NAS Norfolk. At that session it was decided to make the central portion of the insignia be the fierce-

Prior to Operation 'Torch' VF-41's Grumman F4F-4 Wildcats sported large national insignia and a small 'Red Ripper' insignia beneath the cockpit./*US Navy*

looking boar found on the label of a bottle of Gordon's gin. Mounted on a proper shield, it looked fine but lacked more "colour". Hence, the bar sinister in the form of a bolt of lightning was draped over the left shoulder as a sign of bastardy in the manner of ancient nobility. Appropriately, a string of link baloney was added to the bottom to represent the squadron's outstanding "bull session" capabilities. Then, to put the members in proper perspective, two big red balls of fire were incorporated as a sign of masculinity. The whole picture was summed up in a toast that went like this: "Here's to the pilots of Fighting Four,* the best he-man, baloney-slinging, gin-drinking bastards in the Navy!"

'By the end of 1940, when VF-4 received its first production F4Fs, the war had been going on for over a year and, despite America's official neutrality, we felt it was only a matter of time before we would become involved. Consequently, our training took on a special meaning. We were glad to be out of the biplane era, but aware that we had a lot to do to catch up with the warring powers.

'The F4F, for example, was highly prone to ground looping. Although the landing gear tucked up nicely into the fuselage when airborne, the design of the gear resulted in a very narrow tread when the landing gear was extended. The shock struts were so close to the centre line of the aircraft that when one of them compressed an inch, the wing on that side went down a full yard. It was like landing an ice skate.

*When commissioned on 1 February 1927, the squadron was designated VF-5S. The unit was later redesignated VB-1B, then VF-5B, then VF-4 and, early in World War 2, VF-41. Under the unique US Navy squadron designation system, it is now known as VF-11.

'It was said there were two kinds of Wildcat pilots: those who had ground looped and those who were about to do so. I logged my ground loop at NAS Guantanamo Bay, Cuba, where I went off the runway to the left, dragging the *left* wing, contrary to usual experience. One of our pilots ground looped a Wildcat to the right and tore up the left wing only to get the airplane righted and go into a ground loop to the left and tear up the right wing! The Wildcat demanded certain expertise and constant attention.

'The F4F's landing gear was retracted manually by a hand crank which required some 30 turns to bring the gear up. When lowering the gear, the first turn or two unlocked the gear, after which the weight of the gear would spin the crank unless it was manually restrained. If the crank slipped from your grip, it would spin madly and beat your hand black and blue. Then, when the spinning ceased, you had to be careful to give the crank a few more hard turns to ensure that the gear was locked in the "down" position. Otherwise, the gear would collapse on landing and the first part of the airplane to touch the runway would be the fuel pump, which would be immediately ground off, igniting the fuel, all of which would drain into the fire. Since the pilot sat on the main fuel tank, it was in his best interests to exit as quickly as possible.

'Just before we went aboard USS *Ranger* to participate in Operation "Torch", our skipper, Lt-Cdr C.T. ("Tommy") Booth, had a problem with his landing gear. We were operating out of NAS Norfolk and practising dive bombing and, as the skipper pulled out of a dive, his gear broke loose from the up-lock position and extended, carrying away the shock struts. Tommy headed back for Norfolk, anticipating a belly landing with the ensuing fireworks. Much to his great surprise – and relief – when he landed the gear did *not* collapse and he rolled to a nice stop with the struts hanging loose. The landing gear extension geometry was such that it went over centre and jammed in the down position.

'Things began to change in the US Navy as we approached Operation "Torch". For years our squadron was assigned 18 aircraft and 18 pilots, with three or four pilots rotating out each year as replacements reported aboard. The squadron was always heavy with "old hands", which kept us younger and newer pilots on the alert. We flew the same individual aircraft on every flight and if we were directed to fly another man's airplane, we were certainly aware of the "differences", real or imaginary. But as it came time for us to get into combat, all of these events began to change. More of the veteran pilots were transferred out to help with the Navy's expanding training programme, the number of aircraft was increased to 27 and, consequently, many new pilots began to arrive. It was an uncertain and unsettling time and, fortunately, we had a strong leader in Tommy Booth, who worked hard to keep the squadron running smoothly in spite of the disruptions.

'One of our missions before we left for North Africa was to search for German submarines.

This was actually an extension of the old Neutrality Patrols, during which we would go from Bermuda to the Cape Verde Islands, up to the Azores and back to Bermuda. While the scout bombers flew both search and anti-submarine warfare patrols, the fighters were assigned to look for the tell-tale signs of periscopes knifing through the water. These were low-level flights around the Task Force and were probably intended to provide us with flight time to keep up our proficiency. For the first hour I would search diligently for any sign of a submarine, then I would perk up once in awhile during the second hour and be generally ineffective during the third hour.

'On one of these patrols I had settled down into a dull 100kt cruise at 500ft on a nice tropical sunny day. I had a bit of athlete's foot and thought that some warm sun might help. So I took off my shoes and socks and stuck my feet out the side. That felt so good that I took off my life jacket, shirt and undershirt to tan my chest. Then I shucked my trousers and was soon flying only in my undershorts. What a life!

'Suddenly, the carrier was flashing a light signal to me. They were blinking the code word "CAST", which meant to land aboard right

*Below:* Markings used just prior to Operation 'Torch' were the large plain white star on the blue field, as seen in this view of a VF-29 Wildcat aboard USS *Santee* (AVG-29). Fuselage designation '29-GF-4' indicates this F4F-4 was the No 4 aircraft in VF-29 aboard an AVG-type ship./*US Navy*

*Above:* Grumman F4F-4 of VF-29 has its tail ripped off after a hard landing aboard USS *Santee* (AVG-29) during Operation 'Torch'. Aircraft has yellow circle around national insignia and '29-GF-10' markings on fuselage, indicating it was the No 10 aircraft in the squadron./*US Navy*

away. I was directly astern of the *Ranger* so I put down the landing gear and turned into a final approach. I managed to get on my shirt and life jacket before I landed, but that was all. After I came aboard I taxied very smartly past the island superstructure to a parking position forward on the flight deck.

'A firm rule of carrier opeations is that pilots do *not* stay on the flight deck after landing. They get out of their aircraft and go below decks and out of the way. While I was frantically getting into the rest of my clothes, the *Ranger*'s Air Officer was frantically yelling at me on the bullhorn to get the hell out of that airplane. I finally did, but not before I had managed to compose myself before stepping out in front of all of those sailors on the flight deck.

'We went to Bermuda for final training and assembly, and then we joined Task Force 34. During the ocean crossing we were made aware of the forthcoming operation and how important it was to have North Africa in Allied hands. After we saw what "the big picture" was, we concentrated on our own small niche of the operation. In the case of VF-41, that was air operations in the Casablanca area.

'It soon became apparent, however, that we really didn't know much about our proposed area of operations. Of course, we had general maps, but they did not contain specific details of coastlines and landmarks. To rectify that situation, our Air Intelligence people did an excellent job of gathering information from many sources, even locating individual travellers' snapshots. Only one aspect of their work gave me a problem. In their zeal to help us, they prepared local charts and maps oriented in such a way that the *top* of the map was the course they expected us to be on when we arrived to cover the invasion. Very commendable – except that all of our navigational training had been with charts on which *north* is always at the *top*. It is a small point, to be sure, but it had a few of us

in a quandary trying to figure out where we were going.

'We arrived off the coast of North Africa early on the morning of 8 November 1942. It was very peaceful and quiet; it didn't seem to be the sort of place where you could be killed. Even as we took off with the first flight at daybreak, I didn't feel that we would be involved in combat. I felt that the French forces had made their show for the Nazis and now they would simply let us land and join them. So, I still sailed along in hopeful serenity.

'I was rudely shaken out of that mood by a sky full of anti-aircraft bursts. Our own Task Force ships, which were between the carrier and the coast, were sending up everything they had. The battleship USS *Massachusetts* (BB-59) had so many anti-aircraft guns going that it looked as though it were on fire. No one in our formation was hit, but we were scattered around quite a bit and my second section never did get back in place. I was certainly glad that our people down below couldn't shoot any better than they could recognise aircraft types!

'Any hopes for a peaceful reception were dashed once and for all when the code words "Play Ball" were radioed to our flight. That meant that the opposition – it was still hard to think of the French as our enemies – had fired on some of our forces somewhere and that we all would *really* go into combat.

'We had not been trained in "the Thach weave" or any other mutually supportive defensive tactics. Our method of engaging the enemy was like something right out of a World War 1 dogfight: a bunch of us sailing into a bunch of them, with each group trying to do the best they could. We did try to stay together in the same general area so that we would be able to help each other. As soon as we got over the beach, my wingman saw a single target and broke away to go after it. He immediately had an enemy aircraft on his tail, peppering him like mad. I went down after them and managed to get the enemy aircraft off of my wingman's tail. No sooner had this been done than he went after another target by himself and was shot down. He survived that encounter and was repatriated after the battle was over.

'Things slowed down a bit and our formation was relatively intact. Tommy Booth ordered us to tighten up the formation and to follow him on a strafing attack on a French airfield. We came down and swung in toward a line of aircraft that were warming up on the flight line prior to take off. Suddenly there was anti-aircraft fire coming from numerous positions on the ground. To escape that murderous fire I dived down toward a clearing just short of the airfield and behind a grove of trees. As I neared the trees, I pulled up, skimmed over the trees and raked the whole line of aircraft with my four .50 cal machine guns. I still had two racks full of incendiary bombs, which I wanted to get rid of, so I dumped them all as I passed over the lined-up aircraft.

'As I started to pull up, an AA battery across the field began winking at me. I pushed over again and put a burst into it. When I began to pull up again, a larger calibre AA gun in a roofless square mud building opened fire at me. I pushed over again to counter that threat and began to wonder whether I was ever going to get any altitude.

'By this time Tommy Booth was reforming our flight again and because I had been delayed while trying to pull up from the strafing attack, I was still quite a distance below them. My F4F was standing on its tail and I was pouring on the power in a frantic effort to rejoin my friends. I was also busy looking around for any unexpected company, as I recalled the old World War 1 fighter pilot's motto: "Beware the Hun in the sun". I squinted intently into the sun and at first I saw nothing, but then I saw a winged shape coming toward me. When it wavered from the direct line of the sun I quickly recognised it as one of the Curtiss 75A Hawks we had sold the French. He had me boresighted and was just closing the range to fire. I didn't really know just what to do at the moment, so I simply sat there – until the last second before he could open fire. Then I turned toward him as steeply as I could. My turn at a relatively low speed was much tighter than his at a high diving speed, so he could not pull his sights up onto me in the turn. He was never able to fire a shot at me.

'I continued around the turn and my adversary attempted to pull back up after me. Of course, his speed carried him away around, with the result that he zoomed right back up in front of me and now the tables were turned. My turn must have been rather tight because Tommy Booth later asked, "Who was the guy turning on his own tail up there?" In any case, I had a good solid target right in front of me. But, before I could fire, the pilot bailed out and went drifting down in his parachute. That meant I didn't get to – or even *have to* – shoot down another airplane. But it occurred to me that this would be a good opportunity to get some gunsight camera footage of an "aerial victory", so I closed in on the Curtiss 75A and opened fire with my four .50 cal machine guns. That was a mistake. The airplane literally came apart in the air. One landing gear, strut and all, came tumbling back at me and looked as though it would surely come right into the cockpit with me. But it somehow tumbled right over my cockpit canopy and was gone in an instant.

'For a moment I considered going back to get some film of the pilot in his parachute. I left the camera on and switched the guns off and started down. Then the thought came to me that my hapless adversary would think I was going to use the guns on him. So I gave up that idea and gave him a wide berth. As I got near his altitude, I waggled my wings at him and kept right on going.

'By now I had lost all sight of Tommy Booth and the others, and a quick check of the fuel gauge showed I had just about enough gasoline to get back to the carrier. Therefore I headed toward the sea, all alone, bound for the position where I calculated the *Ranger* would be. As I approached the coastline, however, I was suddenly confronted by an enemy fighter, coming at me on a head-on collision course from slightly above. There was *no* way to avoid the attack! All I could do was stay on course and rely on my superior firepower. I put the gunsight "pipper" right on his cockpit and waited for him to come within firing range. We closed rapidly, but, for some reason totally unknown to me I never opened fire. Neither did he. I skimmed underneath him by a few feet and *then* recognised that the aircraft was *not* an enemy fighter. It was one of our own SBD dive bombers. I turned and watched him proceed inland without a waver. He obviously had never even seen me. In a head-on view the Curtiss 75A and the Douglas SBD are nearly identical, except for the landing gear "knuckles" of the Curtiss Hawk, which are not readily visible when the aircraft is seen from slightly below.

'As I continued out to sea, other aircraft began to join up with me individually and in groups of two and three. Apparently, when I headed out to sea, it *appeared* that I knew where I was going. So those shipmates and squadronmates who weren't entirely sure of the *Ranger*'s location simply fell in behind. There was no time to discuss the issue because we all had to find a place to land – and quickly.

'I expected to see something, even smoke on the horizon, as I approached the "point option" where the carrier was supposed to be. But there was nothing. I knew from the radio transmissions that German U-Boats were supposed to be in the area, so it was not too surprising that our ship was not precisely where I expected it to be. Looking around, I spotted a small rain shower to the south and I reasoned that, if I were Captain of the ship and wanted to avoid unwelcome company, I would hide in the rain squall. Consequently, I altered course and led the rag-tag group into the squall and, as it happened, right into *Ranger*'s landing pattern. Once I got back aboard I had barely enough fuel left to jiggle the gauge.'

Although 'Bud' Furney and other Americans expected little more than token resistance from the Vichy French forces, the opposition was indeed quite stiff. At the time of the invasion USS *Ranger* was the only large American aircraft carrier in the Atlantic and therefore a prime target for Axis submarines. On the third day of the invasion, 10 November, *Ranger* did come under torpedo attack – not from German U-Boats but from the French submarine *Tonnant*. The French vessel fired four torpedoes, all of which passed under the carrier's stern. 'Bud' Furney was aboard *Ranger* during the attack and recalls:

'The submarine managed to slip within our destroyer screen and fire its "fish" broadside at us. One of the torpedoes malfunctioned and continuously popped up out of the water like a porpoise. All of the torpedoes passed under the stern – but so close to the ship that the Landing Signal Officer looked down from his platform just off the flight deck and saw them very clearly.

'We continued to fly missions over the beach, hitting enemy targets and looking for enemy fighters. One of my friends, Ens "Dub" Taylor, was on a flight near Casablanca when he chased an enemy fighter into a fog bank, while another was on his tail, hammering away at him. In the fog "Dub" had to rely solely on his instruments and when he saw what a low altimeter reading he had, he got so scared that he just yanked the stick back with both hands. His timing was perfect because at that point his Wildcat mushed into the ground in a nose-up attitude at over 300kts. But "Dub" managed to keep going and climb out of the fog on instruments. He was then all alone and there wasn't a trace of the two planes he had mixed it up with. We think he "got" two victories! He came back aboard USS *Ranger* with the belly antenna ripped off, mud all along the belly, paint cleaned off of the propeller blade tips, and the tail wheel drag link broken. They checked the prop pitch and track, fixed the tail wheel and, a short time later, launched him to go off and try for two more.

'While the hostilities were going on we continued to patrol over Casablanca at 20,000ft. During one such patrol we were told that the seacoast battery at Point El Hank was giving our surfaces a bad time whenever they came in close. The dive bombers were ordered to knock out the battery, but they couldn't really get close because the flak was so heavy. Consequently, the fighters were ordered to strafe just ahead of the dive bombers to force the AA crews to keep their heads down.

'The F4F *would* indicate 475kts in a dive and we proved it on this mission. We flew along at 20,000ft and went almost past the target before we pushed over in a vertical dive that was so steep we almost went over on our backs. We indicated 475kts! Then we rounded out so that the last part of our dive into the AA nests was a very shallow run with a lot of speed. We fired all the way and then retired out over the water, right down on the deck, still indicating over 300kts. We felt safe enough, but a row of AA splashes passed us on the right side. We turned to the left and a row of splashes passed us on that side. So we just headed straight out to sea and trusted to luck. No one was hit, not even any of the dive bombers, who got the battery.

'We resumed our patrol at 20,000ft in a leisurely clear sky with no enemy aircraft in sight. As we went along something on the surface of the water caught my eye. It appeared to be a surfaced submarine, leaving the harbour and heading for our carrier at high speed. I couldn't believe it! I called Tommy Booth, who was leading the other division of four F4Fs, and asked him if he had also seen the submarine. Tommy replied, "Yes, and there's another a bit farther out. You take the inboard one and I'll take the outer one."

'We had to make strafing runs, as we carried no bombs during that mission and the dive bombers had already left us and were too far away to get back in time to hit the submarines. We thought that strafing would at least make them submerge and thereby reduce their speed to about one-fourth of the surface speed or perhaps less. That would give the ship time to prepare for an attack.

'I signalled my division to follow me and then turned 90 degrees into the attack so that they could spread out. Then I pushed over into a dive.

As I neared the target and was almost ready to open fire, a stream of red tracers went past my wing. My first thought was, "Oh God, I've got one on my tail!" But a quick glance showed that it was my own wingman shooting at the submarine. In their eagerness to nail the sub, the other pilots had not really spread out; they had simply pushed over into the dive and spread out just far enough to shoot clear of each other. We wound up with all four of us firing simultaneously. Sixteen .50 cal machine guns loaded with tracer, incendiary and armour-piercing bullets, all hammering away together in a firepower demonstration of substantial proportions.

'After that initial attack, we pulled up and headed back for the *Ranger*. Our patrol time was about up and we were quite certain that we had at least managed to slow down the submarines. When the next patrol returned, we learned just how successful we had been. They reported spotting both submarines on the beach. Apparently, the two subs had been so badly damaged that their respective skippers had to run them aground to save the crews.

'Emboldened by success, on our next mission my three squadron mates and I tried to knock down one of the twin-engine Douglas A-20 Havocs that the French were using. We knew the A-20 could outrun us in level flight, so after we spotted this one, we attempted to sneak up on it from astern. After a while I realised that we were heading full bore for the mountains, inland, and not gaining a bit on the target. We simply didn't have the fuel to play this kind of a game, so we gave up on the A-20 and headed back for the coast at an economical cruising speed. Looking back, I was shocked to see the French bomber following us. I knew we could take him head-on, so I called for a *very* sharp 180-degree turn and full power. Sure enough, our French friend made a 180-degree turn and stayed just out of reach.

We gave up again and headed back toward the coast. He followed us. We ignored him. Then another pair of quick turns and, each time, an A-20 just out of reach. This time we were getting so low on fuel that we had to give up the game – before that damned A-20 "got" four Wildcats without firing a shot!'

For 'Bud' Furney that event was the last hostile action in the skies over North Africa. Furney, who went on to command Air Group 28 aboard USS *Belleau Wood* (CVL-24) and later became the US Navy's 269th jet pilot, received the Navy Cross for his exploits during Operation 'North'. That operation was concluded when Vichy French authorities in Casablanca surrendered to the Americans on 11 November 1942, the 24th anniversary of the armistice that ended World War 1.

During the four-day battle, USS *Ranger* had launched 496 combat sorties. Wildcats from VF-41 that attacked the Rabat and Rabat-Sale airfields, the main outposts of the Vichy French air arm in Morocco, destroyed seven aircraft on the ground at one airfield and 14 bombers on the ground at another. Fighters from VF-9 destroyed seven aircraft at Port Lyautey and strafed four French destroyers just off Casablanca. A total of 16 Vichy French aircraft were shot down by pilots from VF-9 and VF-41 operating from *Ranger* and from VF-29 from USS *Santee*. Moreover, dive bombers from VS-41 aboard *Ranger* permanently silenced the French battleship *Jean Bart*, whose 15in guns had been impeding movements of Task Force 34 ships.

Adding to the Allies' successful invasion of North Africa was the most effective combat use of the Grumman F4F Wildcat in the Atlantic Theatre of Operations and, with many successes and no combat losses, a fine beginning in battle for the 'Red Rippers'.

*Below:* Grumman F4F-4 Wildcat takes off over the water./*US Navy*

# Jeeps at Sea

'The ship was stationed inside the convoy for this
work. The convoys were in columns of five ships
each, with about 700yd between columns. They
left a double space in the middle, in the centre of
which they placed the *Bogue*. The other escort
[vessels] were placed around the convoy in a half
circle. The idea was, if possible, to use our
catapults and to stay in our centre position when
launching our planes so there wouldn't be any
wide separation. As it happened, we had
westerly winds on the East-bound convoy, so we
had to turn around to launch planes and to take
them aboard. Consequently, the separation was
fairly large due to the fact that it was what we
called a high speed convoy – nine knots!'

That commentary by the Air Officer aboard the
US Navy's second escort carrier, USS *Bogue*
(CVE-9), indicates the frustration of providing
ship-based air cover for the vital trans-Atlantic
convoy link, a duty assigned to the smallest size
and slowest of the three types of American
aircraft carriers during World War 2. Initially
proposed to fill the 'air gap' left by the
operational restrictions of land-based aircraft
assigned to protect the convoys, the escort
carriers fared better in other types of operations.
They were produced in greater numbers than the
fleet-type and light carriers combined, and they
became the only American flattops to be
committed in significant numbers to combat in
the Atlantic Theatre of Operations. There, the
escort carriers' duties ranged from hunting
German submarines to supporting ground
operations during the Allied invasion of Europe.

Although American interest in small or light-
class aircraft carriers went back almost to the
dawn of US carrier operations, producing such
ships was not given strong governmental support
until after the war in Europe was in progress for
over a year. On 21 October 1940, the Chief of
Naval Operations, Adm Harold R. Stark, was
ordered by President Franklin D. Roosevelt to
develop plans to use a merchant ship that would
'provide quick conversions for carrying small
planes which could hover ahead of convoys,
detect submarines and drop smoke bombs to
indicate their locations to an attacking surface
escort craft.'

In January 1941, a conference convened by
Adm Stark decided the vessels most suitable for
conversion would be two C-3 cargo ships to be
obtained from the US Maritime Commission.
The ships were diesel-powered to eliminate the
need for smokestacks and, in accordance with
President Roosevelt's charge to the CNO,
conversion was completed within three months.
The first ship selected, the *Mormacmail*, was
acquired on 6 March 1941 and commissioned on
2 June as the US Navy's first aircraft escort
vessel, USS *Long Island* (AVG-1). The ship
displaced 15,400ton fully loaded, had a flight
deck 362ft long and indicated a trial run speed of
17.6kts. Equipped with one elevator, USS *Long
Island* accommodated 16 aircraft, as well as 190
officers and 780 enlisted men. The second C-3
ship, the former *Mormacland*, was acquired at
the same time and completed for the Royal Navy
as HMS *Archer* (BAVG-1). Twenty additional
C-3 hulls available for conversion were divided
equally between the US Navy and the Royal
Navy, thus beginning the programme of rapid
production of an Allied fleet of small aircraft
carriers, with subsequent ships being powered by
conventional oil-fired boilers.

On 20 August 1942 all AVGs were
redesignated auxiliary aircraft carriers (ACVs)
and then, on 15 July 1943, they were officially

*Above:* Early escort carriers had smoke stacks along the aft side of the flight deck to avoid venting exhaust gases over the deck. /*US Navy*

called escort aircraft carriers (CVEs). The ships also gained the nicknames 'pocket aircraft carriers', 'baby flattops' and 'Kaiser carriers'. The latter referred to the largest single run of CVEs, the 50 ships of the 'Casablanca' class which were delivered by mass production specialist Henry J. Kaiser. However the sobriquet most often used for this type of ship was 'jeep carrier', a name inspired by both the rugged little four-wheel drive *General Purpose* military vehicle (abbreviated 'GP' or 'Jeep') and

a popular comic strip character,* whose mutt-like appearance belied his ability to help the strip's nautical hero defeat all of his adversaries. Escort carrier sailors in particular felt that, while their ships may have been small and mutt-like, the 'jeep carriers' were fully capable of dealing with their enemies.

That point was certainly proven during the Battle of the Atlantic, in which CVEs were most successfully used as the centre elements of hunter-killer forces in attacks on German submarines. The first such 'kill' by the US Navy came on 22 May 1943, when Grumman TBF-1 Avengers of composite squadron VC-9 from USS *Bogue* (then ACV-9) attacked and sank the submarine *U-569* in the mid north Atlantic. USS *Bogue* was the first of 11 ships of the class that took its name. Slightly larger than the first escort carrier, the 'Bogue' class ships displaced 15,700ton fully loaded, had a flight deck 495ft long, could carry 30 aircraft and had two elevators. *Bogue* herself was the most successful of the submarine killers, with seven German subs and one Japanese sub to her aircraft's credit

*On 16 March 1936 American cartoonist Elzie C. Segar introduced Eugene the Jeep, a small animal of undetermined origin with supernatural powers, into the newspaper comic strip 'The Thimble Theater' featuring Popeye the Sailor. Popeye remains a popular American comic strip and television cartoon character and Eugene the Jeep still makes occasional appearances.

and two more U-boats attributed to *Bogue* aircraft that were acting in concert with other surface ships.

The next most successful sub killer was *Bogue*'s sister ship, USS *Card* (CVE-11), whose aircraft accounted for eight German submarines. *Card*'s composite squadron, VC-1, was composed of six Grumman F4F-4 Wildcats and 11 TBF-1 Avengers whose typical mode of operation was to spend long hours patrolling the open sea in hopes of catching U-boats on the surface, either while running their diesel engines to recharge the main batteries or to be replenished by so-called 'milch cow' or supply submarines. The fighters would then attack enemy sub crewmen manning outside defensive guns, while the torpedo bombers would prepare to follow up with a run to drop bombs or depth charges.

*Card*-based aircraft sank four U-boats in August 1943 and another four in the month of October. During those two key months of combat activity, two of the busiest days for that 'jeep carrier' were 7 and 8 August 1943, when Lt(jg) A.H. Sallenger, a TBF-1 pilot, attacked four U-Boats, of which one was definitely sunk. His ACA reports for those two days describe the action.

On the morning of 7 August 1943, Sallenger was just over 80 miles out from the carrier, patrolling at 4,500ft altitude at about 150kts. He reported that, at 0946hrs:

'I spotted a large white object bearing 15 degrees on my starboard bow, distance about 12 miles. At first I thought it was a merchant ship, but I soon realised it was two submarines close together, fully surfaced, cruising very slowly with neither wake nor bow wave. The weather was slightly hazy, there was no cloud cover and, as the subs were moving at about 2kts, I manoeuvred to come out of the sun. They were almost abreast of one another, not more than

*Top:* A crewman aboard Lt(jg) A. H. Sallenger's Grumman TBF-1 Avenger took this photograph of the two German submarines following the first attack on 7 August 1943. The submarine *U-117* (foreground) was ultimately sunk by VC-1 aircraft./*US Navy*

*Above:* While the supply submarine *U-117* (foreground) lies dead in the water following Lt(jg) A. H. Sallenger's first attack, the companion vessel, *U-66*, moves forward prior to diving./*US Navy*

*Right:* A crewman aboard a second VC-1 TBF-1, piloted by Lt C. R. Stapler, took this photo of *U-117* just after Stapler dropped a Mk 24 mine alongside the German submarine./*US Navy*

200ft apart. There was no indication that fuelling operations had been or were going to be conducted. The sides of both subs were painted white and seemed to be the same size.

'I made the first attack out of the sun with two Mk 47 depth bombs set at 25ft, selecting the submarine nearest me and slightly astern. [My] speed was 220kts and [I] released at 125ft. The subs were apparently caught unawares and did not open fire with their AA guns till I was about 400yd away. This fire was very intense from both U-Boats, although the plane was not hit.

'The bombs seemed to straddle the U-boat and about three seconds later there were two large explosions, one five to ten feet on the starboard quarter, halfway between the conning tower and the stern, and the other just ahead of the conning tower, 15 to 20ft out. I circled sharply to the left, gaining altitude while the turret gunner strafed and the radioman took pictures. The attacked submarine immediately began to smoke badly, throwing off a dark greyish black smoke. It began making erratic turns in a crazy quilt pattern, trailing a heavy oil slick. I had made a preliminary contact report to the ship before the attack and now made another, giving the bearing and distance. I then cut on my IFF* and climbed to 6,500ft.

'The undamaged submarine apparently tried to aid the one attacked for about 15 minutes and then started to submerge near the damaged one. I immediately dived to attack, meeting heavy AA fire from the damaged U-boat. This fire was particularly noticeable because it was necessary to fly directly by the conning tower at 130kts and at 200ft to drop the Mk 24 mine about 40 seconds after the damaged sub had gone down.

*'Identification Friend or Foe' automatically transmitted radio signal which would be detected by other friendly aircraft to keep Sallenger's aircraft from being mistaken for an enemy aircraft.

*Top:* A Mk 24 mine dropped by Lt(jg) Sallenger on *U-117* during the second run is seen to explode alongside the crippled submarine as *U-66* (left) puts more distance between it and its companion./*US Navy*

*Above:* Sallenger's second mine scores a direct hit on *U-117*, not visible due to the explosion. /*US Navy*

*Left:* Grumman F4F-4 Wildcat from VC-1 aboard USS *Card* (CVE-11) strafes a fleeing German U-boat as Lt(jg) Sallenger (whose crewman took this photo) prepares to make another bombing run before the submarine can submerge./*US Navy*

*Below:* Photo taken from a TBF deployed aboard USS *Bogue* (CVE-9) shows U-boat under attack on 12 June 1943. The German deck crew mans its battle stations as a Mk 17 depth charge explodes alongside the vessel. /*US Navy*

*Below centre:* German U-boat is strafed during US Navy attack in the Battle of the Atlantic. /*US Navy*

*Bottom:* USS *Tulagi* (CVE-72) sails for the Mediterranean to provide air cover for the 1944 invasion of Europe./*US Navy*

'The mine was dropped on the last seen course of the submerged sub, to the starboard and 150yd ahead of the swirl. Although I watched carefully, neither I nor my crew saw any results of the mine drop.

'Then I climbed back to 6,400ft, so the other planes could be vectored to the spot. In about 20 minutes, two TBF-1 and two F4F-4 aircraft arrived and attacked the damaged sub. Eight minutes before the relieving aircraft arrived, the damaged sub made an obvious effort to submerge. For a minute I thought he was gone, but he came back up to a fully surfaced position almost immediately. Watching from my altitude, the sub was still on the surface, [and] was strafed unmercifully by the F4F-4s. About five minutes after the depth bomb attack by the two TBF-1s, the sub, having been steering a very erratic course, seemed to settle slowly, still smoking. About 30 seconds later, the TBFs dropped their Mk 24 mines on either side and ahead of the faint swirl left by the sub. Several minutes later there was another disturbance on the water to starboard and ahead of the last observed position of the U-boat.'

German records subsequently revealed that the attack initiated by Lt(jg) Sallenger resulted in the sinking of *U-117*. The companion submarine, *U-66*, was damaged but managed to elude its pursuers.

Early the following day, 8 August, Sallenger's TBF-1 was accompanied by an F4F-4 piloted by Ens Sprague of VC-1. Sallenger's Grumman Avenger carried two Mk 47 depth bombs set to go off at a depth of 25ft and one Mk 24 mine. Due to the poor visibility caused by heavy overcast with occasional rain squalls, both VC-1 aircraft were flying low, ducking in and out of the base of the clouds.

A little over an hour after they had left USS *Card*, Lt Sallenger reported:

'At about 0811hrs we came out of a cloud flying at 800ft and on my port bow I saw two U-boats not more than a mile or a mile-and-a-half away. They were pretty close together, about 150yd, and on slightly different courses. The nearest was steering [a course of] 340 degrees true and the far one 350 degrees true. When sighted, their decks were awash and there was no bow wave or wake visible, indicating a speed of two to three knots. My course at the time of sighting was 165 degrees true, speed 150kts.

'It all happened so fast that I had no time to advise the ship of the contact before the attack. I had turned on my transmitter to warm it up, figuring on reporting immediately after my first run. I signalled Ens Sprague to attack. He slid under me and we made a split attack on the nearer of the two subs, coming in from bow to stern, the fighter from the port bow, the TBF from the starboard bow.

'Ens Sprague made a beautiful strafing attack, working over the deck and conning tower methodically. When I was a little more than half way in on my attack, range about 1,000yd, my plane was hit by at least one 20mm explosive shell up through the bomb bay into the tunnel compartment. This knocked out my radio, interplane communication and other electrical equipment. Later I learned that the vertical fin

and rudder had also been hit in this barrage. I saw the bomb bay light go out right after the first shell hit. The plane took several more hits in the tunnel and something began to burn in the bomb bay. During this run my speed was about 185kts.

'As a result of the electrical system being out, my bombs did not drop on the first pass. I turned for a second run, coming in this time from the starboard quarter, target angle about 170 degrees. The engine was popping and cutting out during this attack. My speed was reduced to 160kts. During this run, Ens Sprague was working over the other, unattacked sub. Again, he was doing an excellent job, but the enemy AA fire seemed even heavier. On this run, the plane was hit in the left main gas tank at the wing root (it had about 30 gallons in it at the time), tearing a hole about a foot wide and immediately bursting into flames. There were other, less effective hits. I proceeded on and dropped the two depth bombs manually; the bombs, of course, dropped in salvo. I looked back to make sure they exploded, and the explosion seemed to go off right next to the submarine, covering it with water. I'm sure it was a good drop.

'By now my wing tank was burning badly, so I jettisoned the Mk 24 mine, armed, about a half mile ahead of the course of the U-boat. I then turned directly into the wind and landed in the water with flaps up and bomb bay doors open because the hydraulic system had been punctured, making it inoperative.

'The fire in the wing was put out upon landing.

I was unhurt. My gunner, [AMM3c James H.] O'Hagan, popped out of the turret and together we got the rubber boat out. I then realised that Chief Downes was missing.* So I swam to the other side, dived upon and opened the tunnel door. I was halfway into the tunnel when the plane started to settle. I estimate it sank within 30 seconds.

'I saw Ens Sprague going in for another strafing attack while we were inflating the rubber

*ACRM(A) John D. Downes, operating the radio in the TBF's tunnel position, was listed as missing in action and most likely perished with the stricken aircraft.

*Below:* Douglas SBD-3 Dauntless lands aboard escort carrier USS *Charger* (CVE-30)./*US Navy*

*Left:* Vought F4U-4 Corsair, once thought unsuitable for carrier service, was easily catapulted from the small deck of USS *Gilbert Islands* (CVE-107)./*US Navy*

*Below:* Grumman F6F Hellcat catches cable of No 3 barrier after missing arrester cables while landing aboard USS *Matanikau* (CVE-101)./*US Navy*

boat. After that, I don't remember seeing the plane or hearing the engine again.

'After hitting the water, we paddled as fast as we could down wind, thinking one of the U-boats might surface near us. Although we did not realise it at the time, this took us right back over the scene of the action. We actually paddled through a large oil slick that must have been left by the attacked submarine as it submerged. It was so new that we could smell the fresh oil.

'Although I did not see the guns on the U-boat, I believe that each had at least six 20mm. The fire came from a platform aft of the conning tower. The U-boats seemed to recognise the TBF as the striking power and concentrated on it until we had been shot down.

'Ens Sprague did a wonderful job of strafing and, if there was anyone exposed on the decks or conning tower, I know they were hit. This leads me to believe that the guns were either heavily armoured or had some kind of remote control.

'It wasn't until I was picked up that I learned that Ens Sprague had probably been shot down and was missing in the action.'

Despite Lt(jg) A.H. Sallenger's optimistic damage assessment, German records indicate that the two submarines attacked by VC-1, *U-262* and *U-664*, both managed to escape. Other German submarines were not so fortunate. From April 1943 to September 1944, at which point long-range U-boat operations were virtually cut off by the loss of bases on the French coast, aircraft deployed aboard US Navy and Royal Navy escort carriers sank 33 enemy submarines and participated in the destruction of an additional 12 subs in the Atlantic. It is also worthy of note that, during the entire course of the Battle of the Atlantic, only two of the rugged little 'jeep carriers' were sunk by the U-boats they hunted: HMS *Audacity*, converted from the German merchant ship *Hannover* to become the Royal Navy's first CVE, was sunk on the night of 21 December 1941 by the *U-751*. And, USS *Block Island* (CVE-21), a 'Bogue' class carrier, was sunk off the northwest coast of Africa on the night of 29 May 1944 by the *U-549*, which was itself then attacked and sunk by one of *Block Island*'s destroyer escorts.

Appropriately enough, escort carrier-based fighter aircraft took part in both the first and final naval aircraft encounters with the Axis in the Atlantic Theatre of Operations. Grumman F4F-4 Wildcats of VF-29 from USS *Santee* (ACV-29) joined with aircraft from VF-9 and VF-41 from USS *Ranger* (CV-4) in shooting down a total of 16 Vichy French aircraft during Operation 'Torch' from 8-11 November 1942. To save any embarrassment to their Free French allies, the victorious US Navy fighter pilots recorded those 'kills' by painting German swastikas in the customary aerial victory log beneath the cockpit canopy. The first victories over actual German aircraft occurred on 4 October 1943, when Grumman Wildcats of VF-4 from USS *Ranger* shot down a Junkers Ju88 dive bomber and a Heinkel He115 while covering an anti-shipping

*Left:* Grumman F4F Wildcat flips over after engaging crash barrier aboard USS *Solomons* (CVE-67). /US Navy

*This picture:* Some escort carriers were also used to ferry aircraft, in this case to Guian Harbor in the Philippines in May 1945./US Navy

*Above:* Grumman TBF Avenger engages the arresting gear aboard USS *Saginaw Bay* (CVE-82). /US Navy

*Right:* Grumman TBF-1 Avenger in early World War 2 markings. The red and white rudder markings were discontinued on 15 May 1942. /US Navy

strike off Bödo, Norway. The next victories would be scored by 'jeep carrier' pilots whose ships were part of the Allied Aircraft Carrier Force – Task Force 88 – commanded by Rear-Adm Thomas H. Troubridge, RN.

Following up the Allied invasion of France that began on 6 June 1944, the Aircraft Carrier force of seven Royal Navy CVEs and two US Navy CVEs were needed to provide essential long-range air cover for the 15 August landing in southern France. Adm Troubridge took one division (Task Group 88.1), composed of the five escort carriers HMS *Attacker, Emperor, Khedive, Pursuer* and *Searcher*, as well as two anti-aircraft cruisers and seven destroyers. Task Group 88.2 was commanded by American Rear-Adm Calvin T. Durgin, who had been skipper of USS *Ranger* during Operation 'Torch'. For this operation, code-named 'Anvil-Dragoon', Adm Durgin led the British escort carriers HMS *Hunter* and *Stalker*, the 'Casablanca' class ships USS *Kasaan Bay* (CVE-69) and *Tulagi* (CVE-72), two anti-aircraft cruisers and six destroyers.

The two newer American CVEs were the longest and fastest 'jeep carriers' built up to that time. They displaced 10,400ton fully loaded, had a 512ft long flight deck, two elevators, could accommodate up to 30 aircraft (but usually 12 torpedo bombers and 16 fighters), and could attain a speed of 19.3kts. For Operation 'Anvil-Dragoon', however, neither the ships' speed nor large aircraft capacity were of primary importance. Cruising along the Mediterranean coast of France, the carriers launched fighter sweeps to disrupt German railway traffic and to intercept any Luftwaffe aircraft seen heading for the combat zone.

USS *Kasaan Bay*, deploying with the day fighter element of VF-74, began launching Grumman F6F-5 Hellcats at 0730hrs on 15 August. During the next six days, as well as the period 24 to 29 August, the squadron flew 289 sorties and hit a variety of targets. VF-74 brought down two enemy aircraft – a Junkers Ju88 and a Dornier Do217 dive bomber – but lost five of its own pilots, including the Commanding Officer, Lt-Cdr Harry B. Bass, who was shot down while making a strafing run near Chamelet, France on 20 August 1944.

Better luck was experienced by pilots of VOF-1 operating from USS *Tulagi*. The first of three observation fighter squadrons, VOF-1 was primarily intended to fly spotting missions for naval gunfire, with air strikes as a secondary mission. However, the invasion of southern France caused the priorities to be reshuffled.

Led by Lt-Cdr (later Adm) William F. Bringle, VOF-1 aircraft ranged far inland along the Rhone River. During the first few days of their operations, the *Tulagi*-based pilots concentrated on German ground targets. During a tactical reconnaissance during the evening of the fifth day's operations, 19 August, VOF-1 aircraft got into their first aerial encounter with the enemy.

The squadron's ACA report for the day notes: 'Proceeding north on reconnaissance from Valence toward Lyon, two He-111s were observed near Vienne, heading due south at 500 to 800ft. Upon sighting the US aircraft, the He-111s split, one heading north and the other south. Lt Rene E. Poucel and Ens Alfred R. Wood followed and bracketed the northbound plane. Poucel made the first run, a modified high side [attack]. The plane smoked. Wood dove in from 6 o'clock above, opened fire at 1,000ft and fired until the plane burst into flames and crashed. The attacks were concentrated on the [Heinkel bomber's] engines.

'The He-111 fleeing south was jumped by Lt-Cdr John H. Sandor [the squadron's Executive Officer] and Ens David E. Robinson. Robinson made the first run, a modified high side [attack] from above at 3 o'clock. His run started at Approximately 2,000ft, the target being at 700ft. Hits were seen along the fuselage and the starboard engine. The plane started down and crash landed in a field. Robinson strafed, followed by Sandor. The plane burst into flames. The German pilots fleeing the wreckage ran into the field of fire and were cut down.

'The flight resumed its reconnaissance of the area and proceeded south. Another He-111 was sighted just south of Vienne, proceeding north at an altitude of 500 to 700ft. Wood peeled off at 2,000ft and rolled over into a run, attacking [from] above at 6 o'clock. He hit the port engine and then the starboard engine in a deflection shot. Fire started. The plane exploded and crashed in the woods. The pilot [had already] jumped, but no 'chute was seen.

'At Montelimar the flight swooped over the airdrome and one Ju-88 in a revetment was damaged by Lt Poucel.

'Between Nimes and Remoulins 22 trucks, one a large double trailer, were seen along the road [and] covered with branches of trees. Strafing attacks destroyed all. In the same area a train was observed and attacked. The locomotive was destroyed and 10 cars left burning.'

Back aboard USS *Tulagi* the day's work was assessed and Ens Wood was credited with one Heinkel bomber and shared credit for another with Lt Poucel. Lt-Cdr Sandor and Ens Robinson shared credit for the third German bomber.

There were more pilots than aircraft in VOF-1, so it was a general rule that two pilots would

*Below:* Grumman TBF-1 Avengers in the markings approved on 15 May 1942: plain white star in blue ball on both fuselage sides and upper and lower wing surfaces. On 1 February 1943, the national marking was removed from the upper right and lower left wing surfaces./*US Navy*

*Bottom:* Production of Grumman F4F Wildcats was augmented by General Motors-built FM-2 Wildcats, identifiable by the taller rudder. Most FM-2s were assigned to escort carriers and, in the Atlantic, they were decorated in a three-tone gray and white colour scheme – dark gray, light gray, white – as seen in this view. /*US Navy*

share each Hellcat. This arrangement produced the US Navy's only 'near ace' aircraft of the Atlantic Theatre of Operations. Grumman F6F-5 BuNo 58173, in which Ens Wood had attacked two He111s, was flown by another VOF-1 pilot two days later and used to bag two Junkers Ju52 tri-motor transports. Thus, that individual aircraft accounted for three and a half 'kills', which, when rounded off, generously showed *four* swastikas decorating the victory log on the fuselage side below the cockpit.

The VOF-1 ACA report for the afternoon of 21 August 1944 notes:

'The flight was sent out on a fighter bomber attack against a reported motor convoy near La Capelle. Arriving in the area, it was observed that all roads within a 10-mile radius of Remoulins were choked with trucks and vehicles of all types – including tanks – heading north. The flight proceeded to the head of the column near Cannoux and Eagnols, and commenced attacking along the line of march. Rocket, dive bombing and wholesale strafing attacks were made. A depth bomb dropped by Lt Frederick F. Schauffler hit a group of trucks, causing fire and explosions. Several rocket hits on trucks were observed. The pilots believe that a total of 70 trucks destroyed or materially damaged would be a conservative estimate; 30 trucks were seen to burn.

'In the middle of a strafing run, Ens Jack Mooney observed a Ju-88 streaking along the deck and disappearing into a valley, heading in an easterly direction. Before Mooney could recover from his attack and take up pursuit, the enemy aircraft had concealed itself in the mountain area.

'Upon return from the Rhone Valley, Lt(jg) Edward W. Olszewski [flying in F6F-5 BuNo 58173] and Ens Richard V. Yentzer became separated from the balance of the flight and proceeded along the east bank of the river in a southerly direction. North of Orange, three Ju-52s were seen in a vee formation, on the deck flying in a southerly direction. Olszewski and Yentzer immediately bracketed the formation. Olszewski commenced a run on the Number 3 plane, from starboard, a highside [attack] from 3 o'clock, opening fire from 1,000ft, hitting the starboard engine and fuselage. He made a second run from 600ft above, at 4 o'clock, holding fire until forced to pull up over the target. Fire was returned [by the German transport] from a 20mm ring mount topside. The enemy plane fell off on its right wing, went into a skid and crashed into the trees.

'The bracket formation was maintained and the Number 2 plane in the formation was singled out for attack. Yentzer made the first run from port beam, coming in at 9 o'clock, level. [He] opened fire at 1,000ft and continued firing up to 150ft. He executed a wing-over and made a return run from 3 o'clock level. At the same time Olszewski had commenced to cross over and dive in at 5 o'clock from above. He got in a long burst, following the Ju52 as it broke off from formation. He continued to fire until a propeller was seen flying off the enemy aircraft and it went into a violent skid, hitting the ground, digging in a wing and ground-looping through several fences. One person was seen to flee the wreckage. Olszewski followed down strafing. The Ju52 was demolished.

'Yentzer crossed over from his run on plane Number 2 and made a level run on the lead plane from 9 o'clock, opening fire from 1,000ft and continuing [to] fire until pull-up was necessary to avoid collision. Hits were observed in the port engine and fuselage. Yentzer made a flat tight turn right off the deck and made a second run from 9 o'clock. He observed hits, as before. He made the same type turn and a third run from 9 o'clock. The enemy plane crashed, burned and exploded.'

*Right:* Grumman TBF-1 is placed on the catapult bridle of an escort carrier prior to launch. CVEs used letter and numeral combinations to identify early aircraft./*US Navy*

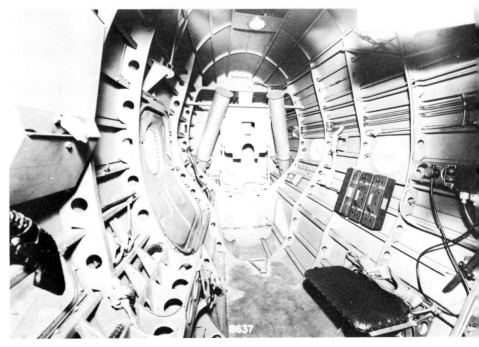

*Left:* The US Navy's only 'near ace' aircraft of the Atlantic Theatre of Operations was Grumman F6F-5 BuNo 58173. Flying this aircraft, Ens Alfred R. Wood (right) shot down two He111s over Lyons, France on 19 August 1944. Two days later, Lt(jg) Edward W. Olszewski (left) flew the same VOF-1 aircraft from USS *Tulagi* (CVE-72) to shoot down two Ju 52s over the Rhone River. */via R. S. Fletcher*

*Below:* TBF bomber's station, looking forward. */Grumman Aerospace*

*Bottom:* TBF bomber's station, looking aft./*Grumman Aerospace*

Ens Yentzer was credited with shooting down one of the Junkers tri-motors and Lt(jg) Olszewski received credit for two aerial victories. When VOF-1 was transferred to the Pacific Theatre of Operations and exchanged their Grumman F6F-5s for General Motors-built FM-2 Wildcats, Olszewski became one of a small band of Navy carrier pilots to record aerial victories in both major combat zones. On 16 April 1945 he shot down a Nakajima B5N 'Kate' carrier-based bomber. During the squadron's Pacific service, incidentally, VOF-1 remained aboard 'jeep carriers', first operating from USS *Wake Island* (CVE-65) and then USS *Marcus Island* (CVE-77).

Also transferred to the Pacific was Rear-Adm Calvin T. Durgin, who, as Commander of the Escort Carrier Force in that theatre, was responsible for refining the role of the small-deck carriers. Under Adm Durgin's command, the 18 escort carriers of Task Group 52.1 played an important role in the pre-assault strikes during the invasion of Okinawa in June 1945. From their restricted operating area south-east of Okinawa, the 'jeep carriers' launched strikes to support the landings and to provide daily close air support for operations ashore until the island was secured on 21 June.

During the United States' involvement in World War 2, a total of 76 CVEs of various classes was produced for the US Navy following acceptance of the first vessel to be converted, USS *Long Island*. Four sister ships to *Long Island* were transferred to the Royal Navy, as were 34 'Bogue' class carriers. In all, four of the Royal Navy's CVEs were sunk, in addition to the one US 'Bogue' class carrier lost in the Atlantic and five 'Casablanca' class ships in the Pacific.

Although the ultimate CVEs – the 23,100ton, 557ft long 'Commencement Bay' class ships – did not see World War 2 service in great numbers, they continued to be ordered during the postwar period. Indeed, carriers of that class saw action during the next American military involvement in the Pacific, the Korean Conflict.

All in all, not a bad record for the hastily-built, mutt-like 'jeeps' of the sea.

# The Mighty Moo

Early American aircraft carrier losses, especially in the Pacific, made it imperative that the US Navy's ship-building programme gave the highest priority to producing more new carriers within the shortest possible time. Merchant ships were already being converted to escort carriers (CVEs) when, on 18 March 1942, the Navy ordered nine light cruiser (CL) hulls already under construction to be completed as aircraft carriers. To distinguish these new flattops from the larger CVs, the nine light carriers were designated CVLs.

The first light carrier commissioned, USS *Independence* (CVL-22) gave its name to the class of ships. It was subsequently joined by: USS *Princeton* (CVL-23), USS *Belleau Wood* (CVL-24), USS *Cowpens* (CVL-25), USS *Monterey* (CVL-26), USS *Langley* (CVL-27), USS *Cabot* (CVL-28), USS *Bataan* (CVL-29) and USS *San Jacinto* (CVL-30). All nine light carriers served in the Pacific and only one of the 'Independence' class ships – USS *Princeton* – was lost in action.

The shorter and narrower flight deck of the 'Independence' class posed certain operational problems, as noted by retired Capt Gaylord B. Brown, a member of VF-25 during the first combat cruise of USS *Cowpens*. He remembers: 'What made it most difficult to operate from a CVL flight deck was its width or, more appropriately, the lack thereof. It was even narrower than a CVE flight deck, as I recall. There were one or two fewer arresting wires, compared to a larger CV, but the shorter landing area did not present any problems.

'Unlike the CVs, whose flight decks ran the length of the hull, the CVLs each had an open, extended fo'c's'le forward of the leading ege of the flight deck which looked like trouble but

wasn't. Even in a light wind, if an airplane were allowed to settle slightly after take off, that happened well after passing over the tip of the bow.'

USS *Cowpens* was named in honour of a famous American Revolutionary War battle during which British troops were defeated at a place called Cowpens in South Carolina. Indeed, the carrier was launched on the 162nd anniversary of that victory, on 17 January 1943. History does not record the derivation of USS *Cowpens*' nickname, but it is safe to assume that the bovine sound of the ship's formal name led to its being dubbed 'The Mighty Moo'. Appropriately, the cartoon image of a truculent-looking cow was applied to the carrier's island superstructure.

Upon completion of sea trials and other combat preparations off the Atlantic coast, the new light carrier was assigned Air Group 25 on 3 July 1943 and began final exercises before heading for combat in the Pacific. Those events are recalled by Capt Gaylord Brown, whose flying career began when he was designated a Naval Aviator on 10 January 1939. He flew Grumman F2F and F3F biplanes and F4F Wildcats during carier operations and served as a shore-based flight instructor prior to being assigned as Executive Officer of VF-25 at NAS Willow Grove, Pennsylvania early in 1943.

Brown was a lieutenant at the time and he remembers:
'The Air Group was to consist of two squadrons, VC-25 with nine SBD dive bombers and nine TBF torpedo bombers, and VF-25, which was to have 12 fighter aircraft of a type to be determined. Lt Cdr Mark A. Grant was on board

*Top:* F6F-3 Hellcat of VF-25 makes high landing aboard USS *Cowpens./US National Archives*

*Above:* Landing Signal Officer aboard USS *Cowpens* throws up his hands in despair as a VF-25 Hellcat misses the arresting wire and heads for the aircraft parked on the forward part of the flight deck./*US National Archives*

'All of VF-25's pilots were on board by early March, although Price and I were the only ones with previous experience in Fleet operations. On 20 March we were notified that a ferry squadron would deliver two new Grumman F6F-3 aircraft to us. Neither Price nor I had ever so much as seen one of the new Hellcats, so we decided to fly up to the Grumman plant at Bethpage, Long Island and have company pilots check us out on the F6F. Then we could simply fly the two back to Willow Grove. But when we arrived at our own hangar early the next morning, the first thing we saw on the flight line were the two F6Fs, which had been delivered late the evening before.

'While the mechanics checked out the airplanes and inventoried the accessories, the skipper and I spent the morning going over the flight manuals and familiarising ourselves with the cockpit. Then, at about 1300hrs, with all hands on the Air Station watching us from the ramp, we roared into the sky.

'What a jewel the Hellcat was to fly! It was so much easier to fly than the old F4F and it landed better than the SNJ. After we had each flown the plane for about an hour, we landed and had a "skull session" with all the squadron pilots. Working with the Flight Officer, Lt Peterson, we developed a check-out programme and schedule of instruction for all pilots.

'Our training continued into April, at which time we were ready to begin live gunnery practice on a towed target. However, since NAS Willow Grove was an in-land airfield, located near a populated area, there was no gunnery range available. Hence, on 6 May, the entire Air Group was moved to NAS Atlantic City, New Jersey, where we could practise aerial gunnery, as well as bombing and torpedo dropping over the ocean.

'We operated briefly from NAS Quonset Point, Rhode Island before returning to NAS Atlantic City in June. Then we sent small groups of pilots down to NAS Norfolk, Virginia for carrier qualifications aboard USS *Charger* (CVE-30). That carrier operated in Chesapeake

as the prospective Commanding Officer of VC-25 and, since he was the senior squadron commander, he was to have the additional duty of Air Group Commander. VF-25's skipper was Lt Bob Price, an old friend of mine from our Aviation Cadet days. He and Mark Grant had served together in VF-3.

'We commissioned the Air Group on 15 February with a total of ten officers on board. VF-25 had four North American SNJ trainers and VC-25 had just begun to receive their SBD and TBF aircraft. As new fighter pilots arrived, we had them log as much time as possible in the SNJ and I worked up a syllabus for formation work and attack tactics involving Vought F4U Corsair aircraft, which we heard we would receive when they became available.

Bay, which had been secured with an anti-submarine net to keep German U-boats from interfering with carrier qualifications.

'On 3 July we flew aboard USS *Cowpens* and remained with her during the subsequent shakedown cruise to the British West Indies. We started off an an eventful note. A few days before our departure from Norfolk – on one of those Sunday mornings that follow a "late" Saturday night – the Air Group Commander went up in his SBD to assist ship's personnel who were calibrating *Cowpens*' radar. This is a boring flight at best and Lt-Cdr Grant, trying to pass the time as comfortably as possible, put the aircraft on automatic pilot, which caused the airplane to "wallow" around a bit. After some time of this motion, he felt the need to unload his stomach and, not having a bag for that purpose, he opened the hatch and let fly over the side. Very quickly, both his upper and lower dentures left his mouth. Since the ship was scheduled to depart in a few days, the NAS Norfolk dental department must be commended for getting Lt-Cdr Grant a new set of dentures in such a timely fashion. The Air Group Commander's dentures again became prominent when we got into combat, as will be noted later on.

'Our trip to Trinidad was uneventful, even though the German government did announce that one of their submarines had "sunk" us en route. We returned to Philadelphia in mid-August and set out for the Pacific at the end of the month. Very little flying was done until after we passed through the Panama Canal to the Pacific. There we conducted frequent flight operations until our arrival in Pearl Harbor on 19 September.

'By the time we arrived in Pearl Harbor, the decision had been made to replace the SBD aircraft on all CVLs with F6Fs. We could fit 12 Hellcats in the same space occupied by nine Dauntlesses. In addition, tests had proven the F6F to be a superior dive bomber, due to the fact that it could carry more weight than the SBD. All F6Fs in the Pacific had already been equipped with two additional bomb racks on the stub

wings, in addition to the centre-line rack for the droppable fuel tank. Therefore, our F6Fs were soon fitted with bomb racks.

'Since Lt-Cdr Mark Grant was to remain as the Air Group Commander, he checked out in the Grumman TBF. Shortly thereafter, VC-25 was redesignated VT-25. There was not enough time, nor available aircraft and pilots, to bring the fighter squadrons aboard the three CVLs then in the Pacific up to a full complement of 24 F6Fs each. Thus it was decided for the time being to split up the 36 F6Fs in Lt-Cdr Edward ("Butch") O'Hare's VF-6 and assign 12 planes and pilots to each of the CVL fighter squadrons. Lt (later Rear-Adm) George Bullard was the Officer-in-Charge of the detachment assigned to VF-25. Incidentally, VF-6 had not been in combat since it was reorganised earlier in the year and, since its carrier, USS *Enterprise*, was being overhauled, the squadron's pilots were very happy to receive these CVL assignments.

'On 29 September 1943, Air Group 25 departed Pearl Harbor aboard USS *Cowpens* for a raid on the Japanese outpost on Wake Island. It also to be our first combat mission. The attacks on Wake Island were conducted over a two-day period, 5 and 6 October. During these attacks, VF-25 flew both strike and Combat Air Patrol (CAP) missions and VT-25 flew both strike and anti-submarine warfare patrol missions. Very little air opposition was encountered, although there were enemy aircraft that got airborne during the strikes. In order to catch the enemy by surprise, the first day's launch was scheduled before dawn and it became very confusing to have four carrier air groups trying to rendezvous in the dark. As a result, the groups were poorly formed and were, in fact, intermingled with one another while proceeding to the target.

'The Air Group Commander was flying a TBF during the Wake strike and, while making a bombing run on enemy installations, his aircraft took so many hits from ground fire that he was forced to land in the water not too far from the island. Lt Cdr Grant made a successful landing and got out of his airplane and into his rubber life

*Above:* VF-25 Hellcat takes off from USS *Cowpens.* Worthy of note is that this 1943 photo shows the earlier fuselage markings ('25-F-9') still in use. */US National Archives*

raft without incident. He was safely settled into the raft and knew that our planes had sighted him, so all he had to do was wait to be picked up by the rescue submarine that was in the area.

'Remembering the loss of his dentures off Norfolk, once Grant got settled into the life raft, he removed his shoes and placed his dentures in one of them, thinking they would be more secure there until needed. After several hours the rescue submarine finally appeared and, being within range of enemy shore batteries and aircraft, the sub crew hurriedly got him aboard and prepared to dive and vacate the area. About this time, Lt-Cdr Grant discovered that he had forgotten both his shoes and his dentures, all of which were still in the raft. The sub skipper resurfaced and the AGC's valuables were retrieved.

'Mark Grant was subsequently reassigned and succeeded as AGC by Lt Bob Price. After a period back in Hawaii, our next operation was in support of the amphibious assault and occupation of Gilbert Islands, including Tarawa and other smaller islands. We departed Pearl Harbor on 10 November and arrived in the operating area on 19 November. In company with USS *Yorktown* and USS *Lexington,* the *Cowpens* assisted in the operation by flying intercept missions north of the combat zone to hit Japanese air strikes launched at night against our northern intercept defence.

'At this time in the Pacific the carrier groups had no night time air defence capability. Only the ships' anti-aircraft guns were available. In an attempt to overcome this serious deficiency, a system of airborne air defence was begun. Under this system each of the three carriers covered a predetermined sector by sending up a TBF with two F6Fs as wingmen during the vulnerable night hours. The TBF would then be vectored to the vicinity of in-coming enemy bombers by the carrier's fighter director. Within a range of eight

miles or so it was hoped the TBF's search radar could pick up the enemy aircraft. Daylight tests had shown that this was marginally possible under ideal conditions of the TBF's search radar. If nothing else, it was hoped that this "presence" would give the enemy pilots another factor to consider when operating in the area. Lt Price and I flew with a TBF piloted by Lt Cottingham, the new skipper of VT-25. Our only claim to fame in the experiment was that all three of us made it safely back from all of these flights.

'It was during one of these flights in this area on 24 November 1943 that Cdr "Butch" O'Hare was lost while flying an F6F. The story I heard was that an enemy bomber attempted to join O'Hare's formation and that caused a lot of shooting by the bomber and the TBF's back seat gunner and that in the confusion O'Hare disappeared either as a result of gunfire or by becoming disoriented. None of our ships was damaged during this period, but I'm not sure whether the "Bat" teams deserve the credit for that.

'We concluded our operations in the Gilbert Islands in December and then returned to Pearl Harbor, where Lt Bullard's VF-6 detachment was reunited with the other two detachments and the new Commanding Officer of the squadron. We were promised replacements and we got them: 12 brand new pilots and 12 beat up old F6Fs. We would have preferred it the other way around. None of the new Ensigns had ever flown an F6F, as they had been carrier qualified in the F4F. So we set up an intensive training programme to give them some general flying experience in the Hellcat, as well as gunnery, night flying and dive bombing practice.

'*Cowpens* left Pearl Harbor on 25 January 1944 and went on to Funafuti, where we rendezvoused with USS *Bunker Hill* (CV-17) and USS *Monterey* along with other support ships set to take part in the amphibious assault on

the Marshall Islands. Air ops began on 29 January and this time we followed the enemy's aircraft to their temporary evacuation field and caught them on the ground. We had received information that the enemy had evacuated large numbers of "Betty" bombers from bases on Kwajalein to a small island about 100 miles north west. Consequently, VF-25 made a pre-dawn launch and arrived with 16 F6Fs over the field just before daybreak. About 15 minutes later there was enough daylight for us to make out the enemy bomber force lined up in neat rows along the runway. For the next half hour we made a series of strafing runs that left them all in flames. On our way back to the ship we sighted about 10 seaplane fighters in the lagoon at Eniwetok atoll. Apparently these aircraft could not be accommodated by the small seaplane base on the atoll, so they were anchored in the lagoon. Again, a series of strafing attacks put the enemy aircraft out of action.

'With the completion of operations in support of the occupation of islands in the Marshalls group, the entire task force retired to anchor in the lagoon of Majuro atoll. While we were at Majuro we were given our next assignment: the first strikes to be conducted against the Japanese facilities at Truk, which were supposed to be very well defended. The strikes were set for 16 and 17 February.

'Air Group 25's first strike consisted of a bombing attack by TBFs, which were escorted by F6Fs. Not knowing what kind of air opposition we would run into, the fighter aircraft were used to protect the bombers from enemy air attacks. Then we went after anti-aircraft guns and covered the bombers during their rendezvous after the attack and on their way home. Japanese aircraft made several attempts to penetrate the bomber formation that I was escorting, but the attempts were feeble and were turned away by our high cover.

'I made two such flights on 16 February and the anti-aircraft fire was the most intense that we had encountered to date. The large-calibre enemy guns would pick us up at about 18,000ft, where we started our run in for bombing and flak suppression. They would follow us right down to our pull-out altitude of about 2,500ft. During our flak suppression runs the fighter aircraft were spread out to divert the gunfire, but even using this procedure my wingman took direct hits by large-calibre gun fire during each of the first strikes on 16 February. I could just see those hits out of the corner of my eye, as each pilot was about 200ft abeam and slightly behind me.

*Top:* VT-25 TBF lands aboard USS *Cowpens./US National Archives*

*Above:* VT-25 TBF Avenger takes off from USS *Cowpens. /US National Archives*

Above: SBD Dauntless lands
aboard USS *Cowpens*.
/*US National Archives*

'Late in the afternoon we were scheduled to crater the fields with long-delay fused bombs scheduled to go off intermittently for periods of up to 12 hours in hopes of denying the enemy the use of the landing fields at night. Fighter aircraft were used for this purpose and each dropped a 1,000lb bomb on a specified field. This was my third flight of the day for a total of 7.3 hours of flying time. During this strike one of my planes received a large-calibre hit in the starboard wing, but the pilot was able to recover and ditch alongside one of our surface ships operating near the islands. Our pilots shot down three aircraft during the raid.

'Upon departure from the area around Truk, the *Cowpens* remained with Task Force 58.3 for a one-day strike and recon of the Mariana Islands. During the run into the area the Task Force was spotted by enemy aircraft and put under heavy enemy air attack for most of the night of 21 February. In fact, some of the enemy aircraft were still in the area and were shot down by the CAP that was launched at daybreak on the 22nd, the day of the strike. *Cowpens* aircraft shot down four of the enemy aircraft.

'We then went back to Pearl Harbor, where we remained until 15 March. Our next target was the island of Palau. It had been determined that since our strike on Truk the enemy had stepped up his use of Palau as a fleet support base and it was hoped that we could not only neutralise the base, but also catch some major Japanese fleet units there. However, the Task Force was detected by enemy aircraft while we were still hundreds of miles away and we came under heavy air attack, primarily at night, which was the only time they could penetrate our air defences. During the period 30 to 31 March our Task Force chased the enemy around the islands of Palau, Yap, Ulithi and Woleai, making air strikes on installations on all of these locations. We arrived back to Majuro on 6 April.

'Our next operation was to provide air support for Gen Douglas MacArthur's forces moving west along the north coast of New Guinea. These operations began on 21 April and enemy resistance was so light that the carrier forces were withdrawn two days later.

'VF-25 hit Truk again on 29 and 30 April before returning to Majuro, where Bob Price and I received our promotions to Lieutenant Commander. *Cowpens* was assigned to Task Group 58.4 – along with the carriers *Essex* and *Langley* and other support ships – for operations against the Mariana Islands that began on 6 June. After participating in the fighter sweep against enemy aircraft and their airfields at Saipan, Tinian and Rota on 11 June, the Task Group took up a position north of Saipan in order to hit fields in that area and interdict aircraft that might be sent down from the islands to the north.

'A large convoy of Japanese cargo ships and destroyers had been sighted north west of Saipan and attacks against this force were launched on 12 June. Fighter and bomber attacks were directed against those ships and the vessels that were not sunk immediately were hit hard enough to stop them dead in the water so they could be sunk later. Anti-aircraft fire from the escorting destroyers was intense and Lt-Cdr Price's plane was hit, forcing him to ditch in the water. He made a successful water landing, but was unable to get his life raft out of the airplane and thus had only the support of his "Mae West" life jacket.'

Other elements of that action are described in the narrative portion of the Air Combat Action report filed the following day:

'Two fighter aircraft took off at 0630hrs and rendezvoused with an OS2U (Kingfisher) from USS *Vincennes* (CL-64) to search for Lt-Cdr Price, who had been forced down at sea during an attack on a convoy approximately 100 miles

*Right:* Group view of VF-22 aboard USS *Cowpens*. Ens James R. Ean is in the second row, fifth from the left./*James E. Ean*

*Below:* Gunsight camera views of the destruction of a 'Zeke' over the Pacific./*US Air Force*

from Pagan Island the previous day. Lt-Cdr Price had last been seen at about 1545hrs on 12 June by a special group of 12 fighters that found him in the water in his life jacket some five and a half hours after he had been shot down. The search planes dropped him a rubber boat and he was seen to climb into it and wave repeatedly as though in good condition.

'The two fighters and the OS2U reached the estimated position of the convoy attack at 0810hrs. Two damaged medium cargo ships, one dead in the water and the other barely underway, were sighted about 10 miles apart. One of the ships had a small boat in tow. There was a great deal of debris in the water. The planes swept the area but did not find Lt-Cdr Price. At about 2345, a "Betty" was observed circling one of the damaged ships. After a brief chase, Lt-Cdr Gaylord Brown and Lt Horace Bolton shot it down, afire in the port wing root, after each had made two flat side runs. The "Betty" broke up in the water without burning, but no survivors were seen.

'After shooting down the "Betty", the search for Lt-Cdr Price was continued until approximately 1005hrs [the following morning] when the OS2U was forced to return to base because of a shortage of gas.* The two fighters were recovered at 1205hrs, each having about 155 gallons of gas left.'

*A postscript to this event took place eight years later, Capt Brown recalls, when he was Commander of Carrier Air Group Seven (CAG-7) at NAS Quonset Point: 'At a party we were telling sea stories and I told about finding Price in his life jacket and our abortive attempt to locate him with the Kingfisher from the cruiser. Cdr Hal Evans, then CO of VA-75, said "CAG, I'll tell you something more about that." I looked at him in surprise and he said, "I was the pilot of that Kingfisher aircraft".'

Although Capt Brown's flight of F6F Hellcats and the cruiser-based Vought OS2U Kingfisher were unable to locate the downed Air Group Commander from USS *Cowpens*, Lt-Cdr Price was later rescued and returned to the carrier. He had, however, spent 11 days in his life raft before being spotted just before sundown by a US Navy early warning radar picket ship. During Price's absence, Brown served as Commanding Officer of VF-25 and as Air Group Commander, since he was senior in rank to the skipper of VT-25.

After a short breather at NAS Jacksonville, Florida, Lt-Cdr Price was ordered back to the USS *Cowpens* as the ship's Air Officer, Capt Brown recalls. 'He was lost over the side during a heavy storm some months later. He had been directing the security of aircraft on the flight deck during a violent storm in which aircraft were being blown about and thrown over the side by the wind, waves and rolling motion of the ship. It was not until the storm had subsided and a muster was taken that it was discovered he was missing.'

Before Lt-Cdr Price was picked up, however, the *Cowpens*' air group became involved in one of the most significant aerial battles of the war in the Pacific: the Marianas Turkey Shoot. While Air Group 25 continued to hit Japanese targets on Iwo Jima and Saipan, events were being shaped that would pit major Japanese air elements against Task Force 58 in decisive battle. Capt Brown remembers:

'On the evening of 18 June, Cdr Bob Neiman, Executive Officer of the *Cowpens*, told me in confidence that the Task Force had received information that indicated the Japanese carrier force would be in a position to launch aircraft against our force and the amphibious forces the next morning. The Task Group's air plan called for continuous CAPs by the fighters from before dawn until dusk. Also, about half of our aircraft and the remaining fighters were to be placed in the highest state of readiness, which meant with

pilots in the cockpits. The TBFs were to be retained below, on the hangar deck, until needed.

'Based on the information I had received from Cdr Neiman, I briefed the pilots of the Air Group on the next day's possibilities. After that I directed my Operations Officer, Lt Peterson, to put me in the lead of the CAP flight due to be launched early the next morning. I also made it clear to him that I wanted to be assigned the one F6F we had with the water injection engine. We had recently received such an aircraft and it gave excellent performance. With this innovation, the pilot could activate a pump that injected a fine spray of water into the engine along with the gasoline. This produced extra horsepower for a short period of time by increasing the volumetric efficiency of the engine.

'My flight of 12 Hellcats was ordered to take station at "angels 20" [20,000ft] as soon as we were rendezvoused. As we were passing above "angels 10" the Fighter Director gave me a vector of 235 degrees and told me to continue to "angels 30" and expect many bogies 90 miles ahead. He also ordered me to take "speed buster", which was top speed. With the Fighter Director continuing to give me slight changes in heading, we reached "angels 30" and continued on for about ten minutes. Then he told me we were getting close and to look sharp.

'We spotted a large formation about five miles out at 11 o'clock high, which was ahead and to our left. I made out the first "tally ho" [identification of enemy aircraft] and turned toward the formation. About the same time I could see other formations of F6Fs on the other side of the enemy and more ahead of them. To avoid confusion, each Task Group had its own Fighter Director, each of which was assigned a different radio frequency.

'By the time my flight got to the enemy formation, which I judged to be between 25 and 30 aircraft, the formation was beginning to break

*Below:* Catapult-launched floatplane variant of the Vought OS2U Kingfisher of the type that rescued Lt-Cdr Price of VF-25./*US Navy*

*Top:* Kawasaki Ki-48-IIa ('Lily') at a captured airfield in the Philippines./*US Air Force*

*Above centre:* Mitsubishi Ki-21-IIa ('Sally') from the Hamamatsu Army Bomber School./*US Navy*

*Above:* Mitsubishi G3M2 Navy Type 96 attack bomber ('Nell')./*US Air Force*

up. Japanese fighter aircraft were escorting the bombers but were at first above the bombers and out of sight. We were at their altitude, however, and as we got into the melee my divisions broke off and we all went after individual targets. By this time it seemed that there were hundreds of F6Fs in the air and the enemy formation was widely scattering. The bombers were diving away and only the fighters remained at our altitude.

'My division was singled out by a couple of "Zekes". My section leader and his wingman – Lt(jg) F.R. Stieglitz and Lt(jg) D.J. McKinley – took one and my wingman, Lt(jg) R.I. Raffman, and I turned into the lead plane. As soon as we turned into him, he broke off and made a climbing turn, with me not too far behind, but out of gun range. As the "Zeke" was climbing rapidly, I hit the water injection switch and closed to within 200ft of him. I flamed him with a couple of bursts. My wingman joined up as I throttled back and levelled off.

'We could still see aircraft below us and, as

there was about a 40 per cent cloud cover from 2,000ft right up to 25,000ft, it was not easy in the haze and at a distance to distinguish our own F6Fs from the enemy fighters. Taking up a course in the general direction of the Task Group, below the broken clouds I spotted a lone airplane circling about two miles ahead. It was immediately clear that if one of our planes had gotten separated from its leader, it would have headed for the carriers – and not be circling. When I came within a mile of the aircraft I was able to identify it as a "Zeke". I splashed him in flames with one burst.'

Brown received full credit for shooting down the second 'Zeke'; he and Raffman each received half credit for shooting down the first 'Zeke'. Meanwhile, other members of VF-25 were busy engaging enemy aircraft. By the time they returned to USS *Cowpens*, the squadron total for the day's activity was nine confirmed kills and three probables. After Lt Stieglitz and McKinley chased a 'Zeke' – without success – at the outset of the fight, they had better luck with a trio of Nakajima B6N ('Jill') carrier-based attack bombers. Their actions are noted in VF-25's ACA narrative:

'They next climbed back to 8,000ft and were told to orbit at 30 miles on a 230-degree heading. Shortly afterwards they were vectored on a 270-degree heading and they sighted three "Jills" in a "V" formation. As the fighters closed, the "Jills" nosed down in the direction of the Task Group. Stieglitz dived on one "Jill" and smoked it; he then pulled away and was last seen in a chandelle. He called the Fighter Director to "scratch one fish", but failed to return and was only credited with a probable. McKinley, meanwhile, followed a "Jill" to 2,500ft, where it rolled over and spun into the water without burning. McKinley then pursued the third "Jill" to within anti-aircraft range astern of the Task Group and shot it down, smoking, low on the water. Both of McKinley's "Jills" carried torpedoes. McKinley estimated their speed in a 30-degree dive at 250kts. While recovering from his second kill at 2,000ft, McKinley was jumped by two "Zekes", but lost them in the clouds. Other *Cowpens* fighters participated in the downing of about six other "Zekes" and one "Judy", but none claimed fatal damage to the enemy planes.'

During the action on 19 June, Lt-Cdr Gaylord Brown led additional fighter sweeps, including one over the island of Rota. He notes that an auxiliary aircraft was located on the island and that 'upon arrival, we found ten to 15 planes that had been moved off the runway and into make-shift concealment areas in the cane fields and brush. There is no doubt that we disabled all of them. They did not all burn, however, probably because they were so low on fuel.'

After that raid, USS *Cowpens* and other support ships in the Task Group retired east of Saipan to refuel and thereby missed being involved in the final pursuit of the Japanese force that capped the American victory in the Battle of the Philippine Sea. Air Group 25 did make strikes against targets on Saipan, Tinian, Rota, Guam and Pagan, and then headed for Hawaii. There, Air Group 25 was transported to Seattle, Washington for reassignment. Gaylord Brown, for example, was assigned as Executive Officer of a Tactical Air Control Unit in the Pacific Amphibious Command. He remained in the Navy as a career officer, retiring as a Captain.

Air Group 22 under the command of Lt-Cdr T.H. Jenkins reported aboard USS *Cowpens* on 30 July 1944 and was aboard the carrier when it sailed on 10 August as part of Task Force 38. At Eniwetok, *Cowpens* joined the carriers *Hornet, Wasp* and *Belleau Wood*, as well as three heavy cruisers and 11 destroyers to make up Task Group 38.1. Three other Task Groups comprised the Fast Carrier Task Force, whose mission was to gain air superiority over Palau and adjacent bases in the Southern Philippines and in Yap. The Fast Carrier Task Force was also charged with neutralising any possible Japanese air support or reinforcement from those bases, to provide air cover for the amphibious missions of Task Force 31 at Palau and Task Force 77 at Morotai and to serve as the intercept force against any Japanese threat of attack. On 29 August, Task Group 38.1 set out for the combat zone.

Grumman F6F-5 Hellcats of VF-22, commanded by Lt Leland Johnson, provided the *Cowpens'* fighter strength. One of the members of the new fighter unit, going into combat for the first time, was James R. Ean. He had begun his naval aviation career as an SBD pilot and then, when a call came for more fighter pilots, he transitioned to the Grumman F4F Wildcat and then the F6F.

'Our training had consisted of flying high and low cover for the "Torpeckers" – as we called the TBF Avengers – while they made their torpedo runs. Throughout my naval career, we continually practised formation flying under almost all circumstances. Yet, when confronted by enemy aircraft for the first time, both Ens W.T. Combs, my wingman, and I pulled out of formation to do our work, which resulted in the destruction of the enemy aircraft,' Ean recalls.

That initial combat took place just over two weeks after the *Cowpens'* second wartime cruise began. Air Group 22 encountered no enemy air opposition during early strikes on 6, 7 and 8 September in the area around Mindinao. Hence,

*Below:* Mitsubishi A6M3 Model 32 ('Zeke') in the markings of the 2nd Kokutai (Naval Air Group). Captured at Buna Field in New Guinea./*US Air Force*

the next series of strikes, set to begin on 12 September, was directed against the tougher enemy strongholds in the Visayan Islands. First contact with Japanese aircraft was made just after 0800hrs on 13 September when 11 VF-22 Hellcats led by Lt C.M. Craig were on a fighter sweep east of Negros.

The ACA narrative relates the action:

'Since no enemy air opposition was encountered over the airfield at Bacalod, the flight made a rocket and strafing attack on the field, destroying two buildings and one airplane. Returning from the attack, the four-plane division led by Lt O.A. Higgins, flying at 5,000ft at 140kts, observed two "Dinahs" about 500ft below at 2 o'clock flying on an opposite course at an estimated speed of 180kts. Lt Higgins and his wingman, Ens F.I. Kelly, attacked and shot down one "Dinah". Meanwhile, the other two planes in the division, led by Ens W.T. Combs with Ens J.R. Ean flying wingman, made a diving turn to starboard after the other "Dinah" and opened fire from 5 to 6 o'clock high into the port engine and wing and cockpit. Ens Ean fired from 3 o'clock high into the starboard wing and cockpit. The "Dinah" made a complete circle, losing altitude, fell off into a steep dive with smoke coming from the port wing and engine, and crashed into the mountains on the island of Negros.'

In October 1944, USS *Cowpens* joined with Task Group 38.1 under the command of Vice-Adm John S. McCain to swing north and hit targets in the Ryukyu Islands and the major Japanese positions on Formosa. On 12 October, James Ean flew one of the eight Hellcats from VF-22 that attacked Reigaryo and Kato airfields on Formosa. Preceding the torpedo aircraft, F6Fs flown by Lt O.A. Higgins and Ens F.I. Kelly shot down an 'Oscar'. While that fight was going on, Ean and his wingman, Ens Combs, went after a 'Zeke', which they damaged and forced to retire.

Three days later Ean was part of a 'Jack Patrol', which he describes as:

'. . . taking perhaps 30 degrees of a 360-degree circle from the centre of the Task Group and providing intensive air cover whenever we thought that enemy snoopers might try to come in under the cloud and too low to be picked up on radar. One fighter would go out with one TBF "Torpecker" which was equipped with the primitive on-board radar then available. Also, the "Torpecker's" rear seat man functioned as the gunner, radar operator and navigator for that aircraft and all of those were valuable services to have if a fight developed.

'On this occasion, however, the "Torpecker" developed some sort of operational problem and had to return to the *Cowpens*. While waiting for either another TBF or another team to come and replace us, I flew this portion of the "pie", as we called it. I was flying along fat, dumb and happy, as the expression goes, and I hadn't even thrown the arming switches on my machine guns. Just

*Above:* Mitsubishi A6M3 Model 32 ('Zeke') in the markings of the Tainan Kokutai (Naval Air Group). Captured at Buna Field in New Guinea./*US Air Force*

then, as I had reached the farthest point of my flight pattern, I encountered a big twin-engined Japanese fighter; it was a charcoal colour overall, which made the red "meatballs" on the wings really stand out. He spotted me about the same time I spotted him and, fortunately, my usual good luck held out and I was able to quickly arm the guns and get ready for a fight. The enemy fighter – of the type we called "Irving" – then made the mistake of turning away to flee. While making that turn, however, he slowed down and in that manoeuvre actually presented me with a larger target. I engaged the water injection for a burst of additional speed because the "Irving" looked like a very fast airplane. I also started firing at him. He caught fire and crashed into the sea.

'I broke radio silence and relayed to the ship the message, "Splash one bogey". When they didn't confirm my message, I repeated it. After receiving no confirmation the second time, I sent the message again. When I returned to the *Cowpens*, however, I received a lot of kidding from my squadron mates, who asked about the "three bogies" I had shot down. It seems they had received my first message – as well as my second and third messages – but were too busy to reply as the CAP directly over the carrier was very busy shooting down seven or more aircraft that had tried to slip through. My own encounter then seemed minor in comparison.'

Shortly after that the tables were turned for Ens James Ean, as he found himself forced to make a water landing, although under more desirable conditions than those of the Nakajima J1N1 he

had splashed on 15 October. During operations back over the Philippines, Ean's Hellcat absorbed considerable punishment from Japanese ground-based anti-aircraft fire. He greatly appreciated the reputation for ruggedness enjoyed by Grumman aircraft, whose factory facilities were affectionately referred to as 'the Grumman iron works'.

Ean recalls:
'There were hits all over the airplane, but none of them really impeded the operation of the Hellcat. It was only when I got out over the water that I discovered that the loss of hydraulic pressure left me unable to lower my tailhook. I probably could have made some sort of a landing back aboard the *Cowpens*, but with that ship's smaller, narrower flight deck there was a very great danger that I might not engage the crash barrier. In that case I might hit the bridge, which would make me very unpopular with the Fly One Officer* and the skipper of the ship. Clearly, the best alternative was to make a controlled water landing.

'So I picked out a nearby destroyer and just settled into the water alongside of it. The ship's crew very quickly had a small boat over the side and had me aboard before I'd had a chance to really get wet. Then came the interesting part of the operation. When it came time to return me to

*US Navy flight decks are divided into three areas: Fly One, forward and catapult area; Fly Two, amidships; and Fly Three, the aft or landing area of an aircraft carrier.

*Below:* F6F catapults from USS *Monterey* (CVL-26) while flight deck crewmen run across the deck to set up the catapult bridle for the next 'cat shot'. In this June 1944 photo, VF-30 markings on the aircraft are limited to small numbers on the fuselage and rudder. /*US Navy*

the *Cowpens*, the destroyer's crew insisted on receiving "ransom" for my return. While the cooks aboard the destroyer could prepare such delicacies as their own bread, they didn't really have the facilities we had aboard the carrier. For example, the food service aboard the carrier could make ice cream for us. That fact was well known and whenever a destroyer picked up a downed pilot, before he was returned to his own ship, the carrier had to "pay off" the rescuer, usually with a quantity of freshly-made ice cream. In my case, the "ransom" was a GI can full of ice cream, which was probably 35 or 40 gallons of the stuff. They ran a "high line" between the carrier and the destroyer, and I sat strapped into a bos'n's chair and didn't move from my captivity until the GI can of ice cream made its way across the high line.'

James Ean was quickly returned to action. On the morning of 26 October, he flew one of the four VF-22 Hellcats that bounced an 'Irving' 60 miles off Catanduantes Island in the Philippines. While dodging barrage balloons near Manila Bay on 14 November, he was part of a four-plane division that shot down a 'Zeke' that crashed into the water.

The winter storm season took its toll on the USS *Cowpens*. On the morning of 18 December the ship was hit by the force of a raging typhoon. Despite the flight deck crew's best efforts to secure aircraft, several were lost over the side. As the storm got worse, one of the Hellcats broke loose and its belly tank split open. Friction produced by sliding back and forth produced a fire on the flight deck and the carrier had to be swung about so the wind would blow the flames seaward. Desperate crewmen finally managed to cut the aircraft's lines and it plunged into the raging seas, carrying with it the ship's Air Officer, Lt-Cdr Robert Price.

In January 1945, USS *Cowpens* came under heavy attack by Japanese suicide aircraft. On the morning of the 21st, eight Hellcats from VF-22 went up after 18 bomb-carrying enemy fighters. Lt C.M. Craig shot down five 'Tojos' during the battle and another division leader, Lt(jg) J.A. Bryce, nailed three 'Tojos' and an 'Oscar'. Every other member of that CAP mission scored to bring VF-22's total for the day to 13 'Tojos', three 'Zekes' and two 'Oscars'.

Air Group 22 was relieved on 6 February 1945. USS *Cowpens* subsequently went back to sea with Air Group 46 led by Cdr C.W. Rooney. The light carrier went into the shipyard for overhaul in March 1945, but returned in May with Air Group 50 aboard and participated in the sinking of the Japanese battleships *Nagato* and *Huruna*, the carier-battleships *Ise* and *Hyuga*, and the cruiser *Oyodo*.

At the end of 22½ months of combat in the Pacific, 'The Mighty Moo' had launched some 2,452 combat sorties, her aircraft had destroyed 108 enemy aircraft in the air and 198 on the ground. In addition, 657ton of bombs and 3,063 rockets had been directed against enemy installations, and 39 enemy merchant ships had been sunk. USS *Cowpens* served on active duty until 1947, when she was placed in the Pacific Reserve Fleet. Never seriously damaged by enemy action, she was ultimately 'done in' by the passage of time and sold for scrap in 1961.

*Below:* This F6F-5 of VF-28 aboard USS *Monterey* (CVL-26) during the 10 October 1944 raid on Okinawa is identified by large numeral on the rudder./*US Navy*

# David McCampbell: Navy Ace of Aces

*Right:* Cdr David McCampbell in his Grumman F6F *Minsi III* after scoring his 30th aerial victory. */US Navy*

*This picture:* Grumman Hellcats of Air Group 20 aboard USS *Enterprise* (CV-6) are prepared for 15 October 1944 launch./*US Navy*

*Above:* F6F-3 instrument panel.
/*Grumman Aerospace*

'In order to be a good fighter pilot,' notes retired Capt David McCampbell, the US Navy's highest scoring fighter ace of all time, 'you've got to be comfortable in the air. You've got to know your airplane and be happy with it. Flying becomes second nature to you. Also, you've got to be a good gunner. You've got to have enough practice at shooting at a target sleeve so you are confident that if you get on an enemy plane you can shoot it down. And you've got to be aggressive. I would say aggressive more than audacious. You must get on the offensive and remain on the offensive as long as you can. Stay off the defensive.'

That philosophy served him well during the seven-month combat cruise in which he shot down 34 enemy aircraft, including nine in one hour-and-a-half long fight. During the same period Air Group 15 under his command shot down 315 aircraft, destroyed 348 Japanese aircraft on the ground and sank some 296,500ton of enemy shipping. Small wonder, therefore, that during its tour of duty in the Pacific, Air Group 15 became known as 'Fabled Fifteen'.

Yet, for Air Group Commander David McCampbell a career in aviation almost ended before it began. A 1933 graduate of the US Naval Academy, McCampbell served in what the élite American naval aviators call 'the blackshoe navy' for the first three years of his career. When he was finally selected for pilot training in June 1937, McCampbell was initially declared unfit for such service due to faulty eyesight and high blood pressure. He managed to have the diagnosis corrected, however, and ten months later was designated a naval aviator.

David McCampbell flew Grumman F3F-1 biplane fighters with the famed 'Red Rippers' of VF-4 deployed aboard USS *Ranger*. Then he was assigned to USS *Wasp* as a Landing Signal Officer (LSO) until that carrier was lost due to enemy action in the South Pacific on 15 September 1942.

McCampbell returned to the United States in late 1942. The following year he was given a squadron command when VF-15 was commissioned at NAS Atlantic City, New Jersey on 1 September 1943. VF-15 was equipped with new Grumman F6F-3 Hellcats and, the naval ace recalls, 'transition to the F6F was no big deal, as I had previously flown F4F Wildcats. But I did go up to Lake Michigan for F6F carrier qualifications aboard USS *Wolverine* (IX-64) and USS *Sable* (IX-81), two Great Lakes passenger boats that were converted to training carriers for use in safer inland waters due to the enemy submarine threat in the Atlantic.'

McCampbell took VF-15 to sea for the first time aboard the newly commissioned USS *Hornet* (CV-12), which was undergoing its shakedown cruise prior to heading for combat in the Pacific. In February 1944 the squadron set out for Hawaii aboard USS *Hornet* and at the same time David McCampbell was, as he puts it, 'booted up' to Air Group Commander.

'I was told in no uncertain terms that my job was to lead air strikes and *not* to participate in so-called VF (fighter) scrambles,' he recalls. As disappointing as it was to finally have a fighter aircraft equal to the vaunted Japanese Zero-sen fighter and be required to avoid initiating contact, McCampbell was a dedicated career officer who understood the value of following orders.

Air Group 15 deployed aboard USS *Essex* (CV-9) on 3 May 1944 and took part in the first strikes against the Marianas Islands later that month. During the raid on Marcus Island on 19 and 20 May, McCampbell led the F6Fs of VF-15, the Curtiss SB2C-3s of VB-15 and the Grumman TBF-1C and General Motors-built TBM-1C aircraft of VT-15. Flying in an F6F-3 which he had allowed his plane captain, E.E. Carroll, to adorn with the name *Monsoon Maiden*, Cdr McCampbell directed Air Group 15 against one set of targets while air groups from USS *Wasp* (CV-18) and the light carrier USS *San Jacinto* (CVL-30) went after other Japanese aircraft and shipping in the area.

*Monsoon Maiden* had to be retired after the second combat mission over Marcus Island and, since David McCampbell was less than enchanted with that name, he chose the nickname for the replacement F6F-3. That aircraft was called *Minsi I* after a former girlfriend. He continued to fly that aircraft during the raids on Marcus and Wake Islands that were part of Vice-Adm Marc Mitscher's plan to draw out the remaining Japanese carrier fleet for the one decisive battle that would break the back of enemy naval aviation.

While Allied troops were landing at the Normandy beaches, on 6 July 1944 in the Pacific, Vice-Adm Mitscher's Task Force 58 was setting out to capture the Marianas. Bases at Guam, Saipan and Tinian would put American land-based bombers much closer to the Japanese homeland.

The action began on 11 June, when Japanese patrol aircraft encountered the heavy American force. Air Group 15 was one of the American elements that swung into action and on this occasion Air Group Commander McCampbell had no choice but to engage the enemy.

The fighter sweep of Saipan and the ensuing combat were described in the official report: 'At 1430hrs the AGC was flying "mattress" [cover] at 10,000ft, three miles south west of Saipan when a "Zeke" dived through the

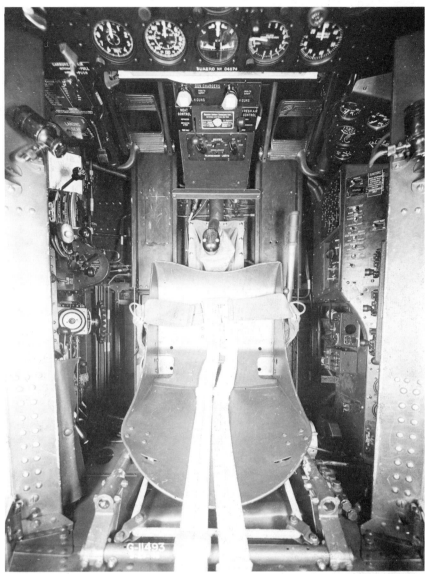

*Above:* F6F-3 cockpit as seen from the top with the seat in. /*Grumman Aerospace*

overcast astern of our fighters. The "Zeke" pulled up in a high wingover on McCampbell's port beam. The AGC made a flipper turn and gave him one short burst, from 700 to 800ft, at the top of the wingover. The "Zeke" made a left wingover, the AGC followed him and gave him another short burst, followed through and got in a burst on his tail. The "Zeke" made another wingover, from which he never recovered. Another F6F in the AGC's combat team, Lt(jg) Rushing, followed him down, firing. McCampbell saw the "Zeke" hit the water, without burning. McCampbell used water injection and although he retained his belly tank, he followed the "Zeke" through successive wingovers without difficulty.'

Recalling that incident 35 years later, David McCampbell noted: 'I was prepared for it, confident that I could get him, and I did on the first pass. It was no great thrill just doing what I had been trained to do.' But he did single out for praise his wingman, Lt(jg) Roy Rushing, who he says was 'without a doubt the quietest, non-talkative pilot in the squadron, but one of the best shots and keenest eyes. He spotted "bogies"

when I missed them and made us a great team in combat.'

While continuing to hit Japanese convoys and other targets at Saipan, Air Group 15 was again involved with enemy aircraft on the morning of 13 June. At 0900hrs Ens Fontaine made a pass at a 'Helen' twin-engine heavy bomber. The bright green and brown Nakajima had pulled away from its pursuer and had almost made good its escape when Cdr McCampbell went after it at high speed, caught up with it and poured a stream of machine gun fire in it. The bomber blew up about 50ft above the water. It was David McCampbell's second confirmed victory.

Two days later he was given 'probable' (but not confirmed) credit for shooting down a 'Zeke' during a fighter sweep on Iwo Jima, but the real action was yet to come.

By daybreak on 19 June, Vice-Adm Jisaburo Ozawa, commander of the First Mobile Fleet, had committed his forces to engaging Vice-Adm Marc Mitscher's Task Force 58. Ozawa had five fleet carriers and four light carriers versus Mitscher's seven cariers (CVs) and eight light carriers. Heeding the lessons of the Battle of Midway, Adm Ozawa considered himself to

have the edge in the form of land-based aircraft in the Marianas, as well as the ability of those bases to service the carrier-based aircraft.

The events of 19 June 1944 have been called the biggest carrier battle in history. To Air Group 15 and the other US units it became known as 'the Marianas Turkey Shoot', a reference to the American frontier method of flushing a covey of turkeys and picking them off one by one.

Land-based aircraft from Guam initiated the battle just after daybreak. At 1037hrs Air Group 15 was scrambled to repel the second attack, a large force reported to be some 160 miles away from the American carriers and support ships. Air Group 15 sighted the group – estimated to be about 50 aircraft, 'Zeke' fighters and 'Judy' dive bombers – some 45 miles from the task force. They were at 12,000-15,000ft altitude, travelling at an estimated speed of 180kts.

Cdr McCampbell's Air Combat Action (ACA) report narrative tells what happened after he led his F6Fs into the enemy formation: 'My first target was a "Judy" on the left flank and approximately half way back in the formation. It was my intention, after completing the run on

*Above:* USS *Essex* (CV-9) underway at sea./*US Navy*

*Right:* USS *Essex* (CV-9) leads a string of aircraft carriers in 1944 Pacific operations./*US Navy*

*Above:* A 'Hamp' of the type engaged by Cdr David McCampbell. This captured aircraft demonstrated the squared wingtips that distinguished the 'Hamp' from the 'Zeke'. /US Air Force

*Top:* A 'Judy' of the type engaged by Cdr David McCampbell. /via R. Mikesh

formation really consisted of two groups, the lower one being laterally displaced by about 1,000yd and about 500 to 800ft below. After my first pass on the leader, with no visible damage observed, pull-out was made below and to the right.

'Deciding it would be easier to concentrate on the port wingman, rather than the leader, my next pass was an above rear run from 7 o'clock, causing the wingman to explode in an envelope of flame. Breaking away down and to the left placed me in position for a below rear run on the leader from 8 o'clock, after which I worked up to his tail and continued to fire until he burned furiously and spiralled downward out of control. During the last bursts on the leader, gun stoppages occurred (in my aircraft). Both port and starboard guns were charged in attempts to clear them before firing again.

'A brief survey of the situation at this point revealed that the formation had been decimated and the attack effectively broken up. One plane, a "Judy", which had apparently been leading the lower formation, because of his position ahead and near alignment with the leader of the high group, offered himself as a target to me; at this time being 4 o'clock down. A modified high speed run was made on him. Only my starboard guns fired on this run, which threw me into a violent skid and early pull-on was made after a short burst. Guns were charged twice again and, since my target pushed over and gained speed, a stern chase ensued. Bursts of my starboard guns alone, before all guns ceased to fire, caused him to burn and pull up into a high wingover before plummeting into the sea. Neither the pilot nor the rear-seat man bailed out before the plane struck the water and distintegrated. While witnessing this crash, further efforts were made to clear the gun stoppages without success and it was naturally assumed that all the ammo had been expended. Acting on this assumption, I returned and orbited over base.'

McCampbell returned to the carrier at 1226hrs. He was credited with shooting down five of the 'Judys', his third through seventh victories, and given 'probable' credit for another 'Judy'. And the new naval ace did not have to wait long for the opportunity to add to his score. At 1423hrs the same day he led 12 F6Fs on a fighter sweep of Guam and Rota to hit some of Vice-Adm Ozawa's shore-based aircraft and installations.

Approaching Guam from the north east, McCampbell's fighters spotted only another group of US Navy aircraft. But that group soon alerted the *Essex*-based aircraft that 'about 40 enemy planes are circling Orote Field . . . some with wheels down, preparatory to landing on the field.'

McCampbell led his own sweep directly to the area and found 'Zekes' in two to four-plane formations under low scattered clouds. His ACA narrative described the fight:
'High speed runs were made with recovery above and the leader was taken under fire by me, was burned and exploded during my second run. My

this plane, to pass under it, retire across the formation and take under fire a plane on the right flank with a low side attack. These plans became upset when the first plane I fired at blew up, practically in my face, and caused a pull-up above the entire formation. I remember being unable to get to the other side fast enough, feeling as though every rear gunner had his fire directed at me.

'My second attack was made on a "Judy" on the right flank of the formation, which burned favorably on one pass and fell away from the formation out of control. (A rather long burst from an above rear to tail position.) Retirement was made below and ahead; my efforts were directed towards retaining as much speed as possible and working myself ahead and into position for an attack on the leader.

'A third pass was made from below rear on a "Judy" which was hit and smoking as he pulled out and down from the formation. Retirement was made by pulling up and to the side, which shortly placed me in position for an above rear run on the leader, who was closely formed with his port wingman, the other wingman trailing somewhat to right rear. While reaching for a favorable position on the leader, it was noted the

*Above:* Catapult-launched Curtiss SOC Seagulls were often used to rescue downed US Navy pilots, as the rugged biplanes could land in the water and return to the Task Force./*US Navy*

wingman attacked the second of these "Zekes" and his plane (the enemy's) was seen smoking after the first pass. After my second attack, pull-out was made in the direction of two "Zekes" then diving and firing on me and my wingman. Since little speed remained for the break-away, the attack was countered by pulling into them. We took the fire of both "Zekes", with the result that my wingman's elevator was shot away and his plane was badly damaged. I received six or seven holes in my tail and wing.

'We successfully eluded further attack by full-speed retirement, during which we took a defensive formation. Due to damage sustained by my wingman, he was unable to attain my speed and, in dropping slightly astern, both "Zekes" began to tail him. I scissored across and took under fire the closest "Zeke", which burned and crashed after the one pass. The other "Zeke" "split-S-ed" and headed for Orote. I instructed my wingman to return to base due to damage to his plane and then I struck out after the remaining "Zeke".

'During the ensuing tail chase this "Zeke" was taken under fire from directly astern, which he attempted to evade by completing the most beautiful slow-roll I have ever seen. It was so perfect that it was not even necessary to change the point of aim or discontinue firing. The plane began to smoke without actually flaming and he dived off toward the field, apparently for an emergency landing. No effort was made to follow or watch his further actions, since I found myself to be the lone F6F. I then proceeded to the assigned rendezvous point for single planes.

'While awaiting another F6F to join on me, I circled over two SOCs (Curtiss float biplanes), which were on the water in the process of rescuing downed pilots from another group. Two F4Us were acting as Combat Air Patrol (CAP) for the rescue planes, but in spite of their efforts, numerous "Zekes" made passes and some strafed both planes. While protecting and aiding the retirement of both SOCs, I was joined by Lt-Cdr Duncan. During this stage I made three or four runs on the attacking "Zekes", without giving chase to any of them.'

Cdr McCampbell brought all of his fighters back aboard *Essex*, where he received credit for his eighth and ninth aerial victories. Four days later, on 23 June, he led an attack on four 'Zekes' flying in a protective 'Lufbery Circle' over Guam's Orote airfield. McCampbell got on the tail of one 'Zeke' and fired at it until it exploded in mid-air. Then he and Ens Claude Plant bagged

another 'Zeke'. McCampbell was credited with one 'Zeke', his tenth victory, and half of the credit for the 'Zeke' that he and Plant shot down.

Air Group 15 was part of the carrier task force that supported the Marianas operations from 6 June to 13 August 1944. During that time the aircraft under McCampbell's command shot down 104 enemy aircraft and destroyed an additional 136 Japanese aircraft on the ground. They also sank 22 ships and demolished 38 more. After that action, USS *Essex* and her air group were granted a two-week rest period at Eniwetok prior to supporting the occupation of Palau with air strikes that began on 29 August.

Air Group 15 was joined by Air Group 19 from USS *Lexington* and Air Group 32 from the light carrier USS *Langley* (CVL-27) in conducting fighter and bomber sweeps over the Philippine Islands. Assigned to hit Cebu and Mactan Island on the morning of 12 September

1944, McCampbell's group heard the *Lexington*'s AGC make a 'bogey' call. Just then, McCampbell's wingman called out the same 'bogey' and the fight was on. By the time it was over, McCampbell had splashed a twin-engine 'Dinah', two 'Zekes' and a 'Jack'. He returned to *Essex* a 14-victory ace.

The following morning McCampbell led a sweep of Air Group 15 and Air Group 19 aircraft over Visayas. When no opposition was encountered, the *Lexington* fighters broke off to cover its incoming strike group. Air Group 15 pushed on to northern Negros, in order to sweep Bacolod airfield.

McCampbell's combat narrative describes the results of the mission:
'As the sweep approached Bacolod airfield, the weather began to close in and it was necessary to drop down to 6,000ft in order to observe the field. The field was seen to have 20-odd planes

parked in revetted and/or camouflaged positions and one "Betty" was in its take off run with a second ready to follow. Before my combat team could get to the field the first "Betty" was airborne and so was immediately taken under fire and destroyed in flames by Lt(jg) Jake Lundin, my second section leader, and Lt-Cdr Duncan, when about two miles south of the field. The "Betty" was bracketed by sections and all members of my combat team made from two to three runs before it finally burst into flames and crashed. Its position low over the water plus our own initial high speed increased the difficulty of making standard runs on it. The second "Betty" was pounced upon by the second combat team and destroyed in flames immediately south of the field by Lt-Cdr Duncan. The third combat team remained at 6,000ft as cover.

'After this short action the flight was rendezvoused and planes on the field were repeatedly strafed by combat teams until just before the attack by the strike group. The sweep had climbed to about 7,000ft and were a little north of the field when the first "tally ho" was made by one of the bombers, then in the process of rendezvousing 10 miles west of the field. We immediately proceeded to the area and engaged numerous enemy planes.

'We were at about 8,000ft when an "Oscar" was sighted at 1 o'clock slightly below. He must have seen us at about the same time and turned into us and made a half-hearted head-on run before pulling out to the right. When in position, I rolled over on him and got off a rather long burst, starting with 3/4 deflection. He burst into flames in the right wingroot and spiralled into the water.

'With my combat team close on me, we started to gain a little altitude and by the time we reached 8,000 to 9,000ft two "Nates" were sighted ahead

*Above left inset:* Kamikaze plane makes a death dive on USS *Essex* (CV-9). It was subsequently shot down by the ship's gunners. /*US Navy*

*Above:* Yokosuka D4Y3 ('Judy') comes down in flames after being hit by gunners aboard USS *Wasp* (CV-18)./*US Navy*

at 10 o'clock up. We turned toward them and continued to climb until they rolled over on us. My position was such that by turning sharply to the left neither "Nate" was able to bear on me. As the first one dove down, I followed and got in a short burst as he started his pull-out, then another as he turned to the left. It started burning in its right wingroot and was soon enveloped in flames as it dived into the bay. Someone in my combat team destroyed the second plane and I saw it hit the water in flames.

'During this action my wingman, Lt(jg) Rushing, became separated from me by reason of having seen a friendly F6F damaged and smoking badly. He called and said that he was accompanying the "sky chicken" back to base. However, the pilot, Ens Brex, was forced to land on the island of Negros, where he was seen by Lt(jg) Rushing to get out of his plane and to wave as if uninjured.

'Shortly, my wingman, Ens McGraw, and I ran onto a lone "Nate" at about our same altitude. After a couple of head-on runs at each other, I managed to beat him to the turn by turning sooner than he and worked onto his tail as he dove away. He was easily overtaken and set afire and crashed into the sea out of control. During this engagement I became separated from my wingman and so called for a rendezvous at 10 miles south of Bacolod airfield. While waiting for my flight to rendezvous, I was attacked from above by a lone "Nate", which I did not see until it was too late to counter. After his pass, he pulled up in front of me and I got in behind but was unable to fire because his excess speed had carried him out of my range. I dropped my belly tank, shifted to low blower and WEP* and tried to climb up to him. It seemed that I was gaining slightly in altitude and distance

when he started a roll-over to make an overhead run on me. I split-S-ed and dived away into a cloud and succeeded in losing him. Although this action seemed to have lasted quite some time, other details are too vague to assemble; however, the following points stand out as significant:

(1) "Nate" is even more manoeuvrable than "Zeke".

(2) "Nate" can outclimb F6F at 110 to 120 knots airspeed.

(3) This "operational student", if he was such, will have no trouble completing the course.

'When I returned to the designated rendezvous area, five "Nates" were circling and tail-chasing overhead at about 12,000ft and no F6Fs were in sight. Although I was alone and below, I felt confident (knowing that I could dive away and into the clouds if necessary) as I tailed in behind and below and I had almost climbed to their level when the leader spied me and turned my way. Since he did not dive on me immediately, I simply held my course and violently rocked my wings, hoping that his recognition was as poor as mine and that he would mistake me for a "friendly". Apparently he did, because he continued on in a lazy climbing circle.

'Presently, he again turned abruptly toward me and again I wobbled my wings. But he wasn't fooled this time and the whole outfit tailed in behind me as I pushed over. While in my dive I saw friendly F6Fs below me and so I immediately turned to drag the procession across in front of them. The melee was on and it seemed that flaming planes were falling all around, during the course of which I got off a long burst from astern at one of the "Nates" as he dived, smoking, into the clouds. Sometime later, after we got smart, rendezvoused and climbed to 12,000ft, we chased another "Nate" into a towering cumulus cloud, but no one got a shot at him. As time and gas were running short, we headed for base and arrived without further incident.'

McCampbell was credited with two 'Nates', an 'Oscar' and a 'probable' on another 'Nate'. As part of the same operation, on the morning of 22 September, McCampbell chased a 'Dinah' over Manila Bay and fired a rocket at the twin-engine Mitsubishi. The rocket did not explode, but it did knock off part of the Japanese aircraft's starboard stabiliser. McCampbell continued to follow, pouring machine gun fire into the 'Dinah', which ultimately broke up into flaming pieces and crashed 10 miles south of Manila Bay.

Two days later, on 24 September, Cdr McCampbell and Lt(jg) Royce L. Nall went after a 'Pete' off the coast of Cebu and soon set fire to the seaplane and caused it to crash. Both pilots shared credit for shooting down the Mitsubishi biplane and, since the destroyed 'Pete' was David McCampbell's second 'half-kill', it brought his score up to 19 enemy aircraft.

As American air elements continued to pound Japanese positions and maritime traffic in the Philippines, softening up that former US protectorate for invasion and recapture, aircraft

*Below:* A 'Dinah' of the type engaged in combat by Cdr David McCampbell./*via R. Mikesh*

from USS *Essex* swung north to hit targets on Formosa. Then Air Group 15 returned to the Philippines for a series of devastating strikes from 11 to 14 October.

A massive air effort covered the US Army's invasion of Leyte on 20 October and the following day Cdr David McCampbell added two more Japanese aircraft to his score. While leading a fighter sweep over Mindoro and northern Visayas, his combat team was attacked by two 'Nates', one of which McCampbell met head-on and then followed into a split-S, firing at the Nakajima fighter until it caught fire and hit the water. Recovering from that encounter, McCampbell 'tally-hoed' a 'Dinah' some 6,000ft above him. After a 12-minute chase, McCampbell set fire to both of the Mitsubishi reconnaissance aircraft's engines. He saw one of the crewmen parachute out of the 'Dinah' seconds before it exploded in a sheet of flame.

The 'Dinah' was McCampbell's 21st aerial victory. It was also the last 'kill' he scored while flying the F6F-5 dubbed *Minsi II*, the replacement for the original *Minsi* which had been damaged during the air battles over Palau. Commenting on his various Grumman Hellcats, the ace noted to the author: '*Minsi II* was what you might call a "lemon" which I flushed as soon as they came out with the F6F-5 with the rocket rails. I got credit for 21 planes with the first two and 13 with *Minsi III*.'

In an attempt to stem the Allied tide, the Japanese committed three separate groups in the Battle of Leyte Gulf, which began on the morning of 24 October 1944. In addition to Vice-Adm Ozawa's Main Body – including the fleet carrier *Zuikaku*, the light carriers *Chitose*, *Chiyoda* and *Zuiho*, and other large combat ships – Vice-Adm Shigeru Fukudome had a day earlier shifted most of the 450 aircraft of his Second Air Fleet from Formosa to the Philippines. The morning of the 24th, Fukudome launched three waves of 50 to 60 aircraft each against Rear-Adm Frederick C. Sherman's Task Force 38.3, the northernmost carrier group, led by the carriers *Essex* and *Lexington* and the light carriers *Princeton* (CVL-23) and *Langley*.

The initial attack was met by Cdr David McCampbell and six other *Essex*-based Hellcats. He recalled:

'Because I was the Air Group Commander, the admiral told me he didn't want me to take part in any scrambles, meaning those times when enemy planes were advancing on the task group and fighters were needed to engage them.

'But this time we had a large group of Japanese coming in on the task force and the word had gone out: "All fighter pilots man your planes." Since there were only seven planes up and available at that time, I called the Air Officer on the squawk box and asked him if that meant me too. And he said yes. So, I started strapping on my parachute harness and shortly thereafter the Air Officer called back and said, "No, you can't go on this flight." And I said, "But my plane is already up on deck. It's being gassed now." So, he said, "Wait a minute." He went to the captain of the ship (Capt Carlos W. Wieber) and asked

*Top:* Cdr David McCampbell's earlier Hellcat, *Minsi II*, being overhauled on the flight deck of USS *Essex* (CV-9)./*US Navy*

*Above:* Flight deck crewman removes wheel chocks from a Grumman Hellcat preparing to make a deck launch from an 'Essex' class carrier. /*Grumman Aerospace*

him. The captain said, "Yes, by all means, with only seven planes available, we've got to intercept this Japanese flight."

'I dashed up to my plane and the crew was still gassing it. The word came down over the bullhorn from the Air Officer to send the Air Group Commander down below if the plane was not ready to go. So I told the gas detail to clear out, although I knew I didn't have my tanks full.'

McCampbell's ACA report provides the details of the hour-and-a-half long air fight in which he definitely shot down nine Japanese aircraft and 'probably' got two more, which were not officially confirmed. McCampbell's combat narrative:

'When on station over base at 0821hrs, a report was made and a vector of 300 degrees, distance 38 miles was received from our own fighter director base.* The last vector received was 360 degrees, 25 miles and at 0833 a large group of planes was sighted at 12 o'clock "up" and "down", which, because of the disposition, had every appearance of being one of our own strike groups. Shortly thereafter, the planes were definitely identified as enemy and so reported to be composed of at least 60 "rats", "hawks" and "fish" [fighters, bombers and torpedo aircraft].

'Since there were many "rats" above our altitude (14,000ft), we immediately started

*The fighter director, John Connally, later went on to prominence in American politics. He was Governor of Texas, Secretary of the Navy and Secretary of the Treasury. Capt McCampbell wrote to the author: 'When I realised that Roy Rushing and I had to take care of about 40 Japs, I asked Connally to send some help. He said, "99 Rebel, we are exhausted of fighters and can't send any help." I then called back and asked, "What do you suggest?" He came back with, "Use your own discretion." So, Roy and I did what we had been trained to do – we attacked.'

climbing. At about the same time the enemy formation reversed course, causing them to string out behind. At this time my second combat team was ordered to attack the stragglers from the rear and informed that my combat team would start "working them over" from the top down. Due to the nature of the "scramble", in which my second section leader failed to take off, plus the fact that we had to shift communications channels, five fighters went down with the second combat team leader, leaving only my wingman, Lt(jg) R.W. Rushing, and myself topside.

'The attack by the two components of my flight commenced almost simultaneously, which action caused the "hawks" and "fish" to dive down through the overcast in an attempt to escape. After Rushing and I made three or four passes, the "rats", having lost sight of their escorts, commenced to orbit in a large, orderly and well-formed Lufbery Circle, over which my wingman and I were unable to find an opening to attack. Realising that they had lost their escort and probably were not too flush with fuel, we decided to maintain our altitude advantage and await their departure, as a result of which there was bound to be confusion and "easy pickings" amongst the stragglers. There was!

'During the next half hour or so we followed the formation of weaving fighters and took advantage of every opportunity to knock down those who: (1) attempted to climb up to our altitude, (2) scissored outside of the support of the others, (3) straggled, and (4) became too eager and came up at us singly. In all, we made 18 to 20 passes, being very careful not to expose ourselves and to conserve ammunition by withholding fire until within very close range.

'After a half hour or so and amidst much screaming for help, the third pilot [Lt(jg) Albert C. Slack] joined us [and] we were able to attack

larger groups. On two passes that I remember, we flamed three planes each time. There were three kinds of enemy fighters in the formation. "Zekes" predominated, with a few "Oscars" and "Hamps". Most of the fighters carried what appeared to be a 550lb bomb, either on the starboard wing or under the belly. The enemy aircraft remained in one large though loosely formed group (excepting the flamers) as they proceeded toward Manila and continued to lose altitude all the way. There were 18 enemy aircraft left in formation when we finally broke off. It was simply a question of watching for an opening, knocking them down, converting the speed we had obtained in the dive into altitude and then waiting for a couple more to "lay themselves open".

'My claim of nine planes detroyed includes only those that were seen by my wingman and myself to flame or explode. Numerous others were seen with engines smoking and diving away, two of which were spinning, apparently out of control, toward the water and are claimed as probables. Others were hit and undoubtedly damaged. No attempt was made at the time to record types and angles of attacks; in fact, it was not until we had destroyed five planes and business was beginning to get good that I decided to keep a box score by marking on my instrument panel with a pencil.

'Best estimate of types destroyed by Lt(jg) Rushing and myself is nine "Zekes", three "Hamps" and three "Oscars".

'During the ensuing action, our third pilot became separated and since he had exhausted his ammunition, returned to base independently. My wingman and I stuck together throughout the entire hour and 35 minutes of combat and when forced to break off the engagement, due to shortage of fuel and ammunition, we returned to base together.'

The narrative continues three decades later, when McCampbell recalled:

'When I got back to my carrier that day, *Essex* couldn't take me, as she had a deck full of planes. So, it was either land aboard *Langley* or in the water. I figured I had less than five gallons of gas, hardly enough for another pass. When I came out of the arresting gear, the engine coughed and quit. I was so low on fuel that in a three-point attitude the engine wasn't getting enough fuel.

'After I got back to my ship I had to pay the

*Above:* Line-up of Grumman F6F-3 Hellcats waiting to be deck launched from an 'Essex' class carrier./*Grumman Aerospace*

*This picture:* USS *Langley* (CVL-27), the carrier Cdr David McCampbell was forced to land aboard following his epic air fight during the 'Marianas Turkey Shoot'./*US Navy*

price. The admiral sent for me. I told him how I had gotten the Air Boss's permission for the flight. He said, "All right, McCampbell, but don't let it happen again." Naturally, having shot down nine airplanes on one flight, it never did happen again.

'The 24th was a big day. But the 25th was equally as big for me, since I was designated by Vice-Adm Marc Mitscher [commander of the Fast Carrier Task Force] as a target coordinator to lead three task groups to attack the northern Japanese force, which had been sighted earlier that morning. It turned out that the enemy force was only about 100 miles from our ships when it was sighted. We were circling out there about 50 miles when I got word of their direction and location. I just headed for them and all the other planes followed me. The Japanese force consisted of four aircraft carriers and two converted battleships. I believe there were also four cruisers and about eight or nine destroyers.

'The fight went on all day from early morning until dusk. I was in the air three and a half hours on one flight alone. I don't say the planes I was acting as target coordinator for did all the damage that day, but we sank four carriers, one cruiser and two destroyers and damaged the two battleships.'

Following the Battle of Leyte Gulf, Air Group 15 remained in the area and continued to hit targets in the Luzon, Manila and Ormac Bay area. On 5 November, Cdr McCampbell scored his last multiple victory when he shot down a 'Val' over Subic Bay and then, over land, a 'Zeke' which dove straight into the ground and exploded. He shot down an 'Oscar' six days later and, on the morning of 14 November 1944, scored the 34th and final aerial victory of his career. His ACA report records the events of that day:

'While acting as target coordinator over Manila Bay, I ordered my accompanying photo plane to take a damage assessment photo of ships inside

the breakwater. During this run my wingman and I dropped down to cover the photo plane. As we were losing altitude and paralleling the photo run, we "tally-hoed" two "Oscars" at 8 o'clock, on the same level, on a converging course. We immediately turned into them. The leading "Oscar" dove down and passed under and out of sight before I could bear on him, so I lined up the second "Oscar". One long burst from 2 o'clock through 6 o'clock with hits in the wingroots and fuselage caused him to dive away to the right. As I turned to follow, another "Oscar" passed close overhead and then I saw about six more above us. I called to my wingman, who was astern of me, and told him I was going to make a run. We nosed over to pick up speed. With full throttle and WEP, we easily outdistanced the "Oscars" before any got a shot at us.

'While retiring at high speed we met a "Judy" at our same level and nearly head-on. I took a crack at him without stopping to note the results. The photo plane and his wingman rendezvoused with us shortly thereafter.

'Proceeding toward Laguna de Bay, we "tally-hoed" an "Oscar" at 2 o'clock down. We turned into him and, as my first burst hit him, he split-S-ed. While following him in a steep spiral, I got off a long burst from dead astern before I had to pull out to keep from over-running. Since the plane never recovered from the spiral and crashed to earth in a burst of flame, it is quite possible that my first burst of fire had killed the pilot. The only difficulty encountered in following his spiral was the tendency to dive faster and hence over-run him. After this brief action I rendezvoused with my combat team and continued on my mission as target coordinator.'

Air Group 15's final operations off the Philippines lasted a little over a month.

'Fabulous Fifteen' flew 1,829 sorties, during which 138 Japanese aircraft were shot down and another 117 were destroyed on the ground. Five warships and 22 other ships were sunk, while a total of 71 other ships were probably sunk or damaged.

The entire unit was awarded the Presidential Unit Citation and its commander was singled out for special honours. At ceremonies in the White House in Washington, DC, Cdr David McCampbell was presented with the Medal of Honor by President Franklin D. Roosevelt. McCampbell's actions on 19 June and 24 October were cited as the 'conspicuous gallantry and intrepidity at the risk of his life above and beyond the call of duty' that led to the highest American military honour.

The 34-year old ace with 34 aerial victories to his credit also received the next four highest American military awards. The Navy Cross was awarded for the 'extraordinary heroism and skill' he displayed on 25 October 1944. The Silver Star recognised McCampbell's actions on 12 September. The Legion of Merit was awarded for his role in the operations on 11 to 14 November. And, the Distinguished Flying Cross, with two gold stars in lieu of subsequent awards, honoured the Air Group Commander's achievements from May through September.

Looking back on his achievements, retired Capt David McCampbell still recalls the few simple rules that led him to become the US Navy's ace of aces: 'The two biggest concerns of a fighter pilot in combat are whether he's going to run out of ammo or gas, or both, before he gets the job done. I conserved gas by not charging around at full speed and, as far as ammo was concerned, I had been in combat long enough to know that you fired your guns in short bursts instead of long ones.'

*Above:* Grumman TBF Avenger in the markings assigned on 7 October 1944 to all aircraft aboard USS *Essex* (CV-9)./*US Navy*

F6F Hellcat from VF-1 prepares for take-off. Well known insignia of the 'Top Hatters' is seen under the forward canopy./*US Navy*

# Night Fighter

When he reported to the Operational Training Command in late 1943, Lt George L. Cassell was well qualified for the US Navy's newly expanded night fighter pilot training programme. The Southern Methodist University graduate had entered the Navy in July 1941 and, after receiving his naval aviator's wings on 14 March 1942, he went on to serve as a primary flight instructor for over a year. Cassell had over 2,000 hours of instructor time in his logbook when he was accepted for further training as a fighter pilot at NAS Vero Beach, Florida, where the Navy was also developing a night fighter training programme.

Now a retired rear admiral, George Cassell recalls: 'I decided that, instead of finishing the first part of the programme and going to the Fleet as a day fighter trainee, I would remain at Vero Beach and complete the night fighter training programme. I had no trouble getting into that programme, because they weren't looking for newly designated pilots; rather, they wanted pilots with some flight time under their belts and some experience in the Navy. Of course, what they really wanted were people who had been instrument instructors because night flying is basically instrument flying, but they would also accept generally experienced pilots.'

Adm Cassell was a member of the first group of fighter pilot trainees at NAS Vero Beach. His training began in January 1944 and lasted into the month of April, covering both daytime and nighttime operations. 'The day fighter training consisted basically of familiarisation with the large new service-type fighter, the Grumman F6F Hellcat,' he says. 'Then we went into night flying. In addition to the usual familiarisation and tactics, we practised Ground Controlled

*Above left:* Lt George L. Cassell in the cockpit of his Grumman F6F-5N aboard USS *Yorktown* (CV-10)./*Rear-Adm G. L. Cassell*

*Left:* Wartime camouflage applied to 'Essex' class carriers is seen in this view of USS *Yorktown* (CV-10) at anchor./*US Navy*

*Above:* Recovered aircraft are spotted on the forward portion of the flight deck of USS *Yorktown* (CV-10) as other aircraft prepare to land./*US Navy*

Intercept (GCI) using a piece of primitive Army radar equipment that was available. There was also a lot of overwater navigation at night, which would prove useful once we got to the Pacific.'

Cassell and his comrades continued in the programme until they logged about 80 hours of night flying, in addition to their 80 hours of daytime flying. With a combined time of over 150 hours in the F6F, they were ready for a Fleet assignment. The final preparation came in April, when the night fighter trainees from Vero Beach were sent to the Naval Auxiliary Air Station at Charlestown, Rhode Island. That facility was near NAS Quonset Point, where the US Navy's first night fighter squadron, VF(N)-75, had been commissioned on 1 April 1943 under the command of Cdr W.J. ('Gus') Widhelm. The same unit, which was land-based, scored its first kill on 31 October 1943, when Lt H.D. O'Neil destroyed a "Betty" during a night attack off Vella Lavella in the Solomon Islands.

As night fighter training was further developed, the Rhode Island bases showed continual improvement. Adm Cassell notes that by the time his group arrived at NAAS Charlestown, it was:
'The only station in the Navy that had been thoroughly modified for night training. All lights

visible at night were red and the hangar doors were shrouded with big canvas covers to permit ventilation, but to keep out extraneous light. The profusion of red light ensured that the pilots' night adaptation would not be affected and their night vision would be at its peak.

'At Charlestown we were formed into fleet tactical units. At this point it had not yet been determined whether the growing numbers of new night fighter pilots would be assigned to aircraft carriers devoted exclusively to nighttime operations or to detachments to be deployed aboard the carriers then in combat. Consequently, as an expedient we were formed into night fighter squadrons. There already were squadrons designated VF(N)-101 -102, -103 and -104, and they were either shore-based or went aboard USS *Independence* (CVL-22) on an experimental basis.

'Our group at Charlestown was used to make up some of the first units that could go aboard ship either as squadrons or detachments.* Initially, we became the squadrons VF(N)-105,

*The US Navy's first night carrier air group, CVLG(N)-43, was commissioned at NAAS Charlestown on 24 August 1944. The component squadrons, also commissioned that day, were VF(N)-43 and the first night torpedo squadron, VT(N)-43.

*Left:* F6F-3 Hellcat of VF-9 from 1943 war cruise of USS *Yorktown* (CV-10) approaches formation of other US Navy aircraft. The 'double nuts' (00) on the fuselage indicate this aircraft was flown by the Air Group Commander. /*Grumman Aerospace*

*Above:* Grumman F6F-5N of the type flown by Lt George Cassell aboard USS *Yorktown* (CV-10). /*Grumman Aerospace*

-106 and -107. In my own case, I was assigned to VF(N)-105, which was commanded by Lt Cdr Dale K. Peterson. I think he had hoped to have all "second tour" people, that is, pilots who had either been instructors or who had had a previous tour of Fleet duty. But less than half the squadron was made up of those people. The rest were "fresh caught nuggets", or newly designated Ensigns.

'We trained as a squadron and, since we had had limited training in weapons, there was much emphasis on day and night gunnery and bombing. In the daytime you can see your target, but in night bombing, for example, you identify the target on the radar screen, determine the necessary vector and altitude to fly and, hopefully, tell the point when the bomb should be released. That method was never very accurate.

'While we were at Charlestown we also made our night carrier qualification flights, which ws quite a harrowing experience. VF(N)-105 was assigned to qualify aboard USS *Mission Bay* (CVE-59), an escort carrier that operated in the Narragansett Bay area to work with squadrons training for Fleet assignments. We each had to make 20 daylight landings aboard the carrier

before we could begin our night qualifications. It was cold, miserable and foggy during the March and April timeframe in which we carried out these flights and, adding to the raw New England weather was the small size of the "jeep carrier" flight deck on which we had to land what seemed like an awfully big airplane. Our operational losses were not catastrophic, but we did lose one or two pilots while we were training for our nighttime mission.

'When we completed our work at Charlestown, in July 1944 the whole squadron flew cross-country to NAS Alameda, California. There we loaded aboard USS *Thetis Bay* (CVE-90), which simply transported us to NAS Barber's Point in Hawaii. Barber's Point had all of the night flying facilities that we had had at Charlestown – and the weather was one hell of a lot better!

'Before VF(N)-105 could go to sea, however, the squadron was decommissioned. It had been decided to break up our squadron and form four night fighter detachments for deployment on four different carriers. The four senior men in VF(N)-105 – the Commanding Officer, Executive Officer, myself as Operations Officer, and another officer – were each given a

*Left:* Radar screen of the F6F-5N is seen in this technical manual view of the Hellcat night fighter's cockpit lay-out. /*Grumman Aerospace*

*Below:* Two F6F-5N night fighters attached to VF-80 aboard USS *Ticonderoga* (CV-14) lead a Hellcat parade toward the carrier's catapults for take-off./*US Navy*

*Right:* F6F Hellcat on the port catapult of USS *Yorktown* (CV-10) prior to take off during attack by Japanese aircraft./*US Navy*

detachment. My detachment consisted of four airplanes, five pilots (including myself), a radar maintenance officer and a fighter director officer. It was very important that each detachment work with its own fighter director officer, whose voice they could recognise while working at night. It's nice to know that the fellow you're talking to is somebody you've worked with. We also had 12 sailors for maintenance, ordnance and electronic duties.

'In late August, I was ordered to take the detachment to the island of Maui, where Air Group 3 was getting ready for its next deployment. Since ours was also a fighter mission, we were attached to the Air Group's fighter squadron, VF-3, which was commanded by Lt-Cdr "Willie" Lamberson. We flew with them on all missions involving group and squadron tactics.

'We flew aboard USS *Yorktown* (CV-10) in September and sailed for Ulithi Lagoon to rendezvous with Task Force 58. We had just missed the Second Battle of the Philippine Sea, but we did take part in strikes on Japanese shipping in Ormoc Bay in November. We hit a number of transports that were taking Japanese troops out to fight against Gen Douglas MacArthur's forces in Luzon.

'There was not too much Japanese air activity at night, especially after Japanese air elements had been so badly mauled during the "Marianas Turkey Shoot". Although we did fly night CAP missions, there was a great reluctance to use us at night. The ship was not configured to handle night fighters, the problem being that if you were launched at 2200 or 2300hrs and you were recovered at 0200hrs the following day, it would place a considerable burden on the ship. All of

the daytime aircraft that had been recovered before the night CAP launch were being rearmed and refueled in readiness for the next day's strike. Since they were all spotted aft on the flight deck, in order to recover the night CAP aircraft, all the strike aircraft would have to be spotted forward. Given the wartime conditions of black-out, rain squalls and pitching deck, this was an operation the ship's Air Boss avoided at almost any cost. All of those aircraft would have had to be moved by manpower; you don't start engines at night and taxi them forward. Invariably the flight deck "plane pushers"

managed to push one or two aircraft into each other, damaging ailerons, elevators or rudders. Consequently, we night fighters weren't launched unless it was absolutely necessary.

'On one occasion I was launched at 2300hrs to look for a Japanese bogie that never appeared. However, I was not recovered until *after* the first strike had been launched the following morning. I spent seven hours and 45 minutes in the air. Of course, the F6F could go for almost nine hours when you cut the engine back to about 1,500rpm, carried about 30in of manifold pressure and drained the auxiliary fuel tank. However, your bottom got so sore you were reaching physical limitations before you ran out of fuel! And there was no thought of shortening the flight. On night CAPs we were under positive control of the ship's radar and we just orbited the carrier. They didn't want to send us out at high power unless they had a real threat, because at high power our time in the air would be shortened and we might have to be recovered to refuel and continue the mission.'

In addition to the tribulations of actual night flight, there were other hardships that had to be endured by the night fighter detachment aboard USS *Yorktown*. Adm Cassell recalls:
'Life at night aboard the carrier was interesting. Everyone else worked during the daytime and they were going to sleep when we were going to work and vice versa. Consequently, it was almost impossible for our people to sleep aboard a carrier that was not dedicated to night flying. Even as a Lieutenant, I was in a stateroom with five or six other officers who were on schedules different from my own. I suppose it was worse for the Ensigns or Jay-Gees, [Navy slang for

Lieutenant (junior grade), abbreviated Lt(jg), hence "Jay-Gee".] who were in the Junior Officers' Bunkroom – or, as we called it, "boys' town" – made up of 40 or 50 young men with a variety of potentially anti-social habits. We couldn't take a shower at night because the water was turned off from Taps at 2200hrs until Reveille at 0400hrs. Food service in the Ward Room wasn't geared to our type of life and, in general, we had to get along the best we could.

'We did not have a really good lighting system to assist night carrier landings. The Landing Signal Officer used two flashlights that were fitted with long translucent lenses called "wands". And you really had to look hard just to see the LSO, as well as his signalling devices. Then, once you made it back to the carrier, each ship had its own method of giving taxi directions. One particularly good method was used by plane handlers aboard USS *Yorktown*. They had small, battery-powered lights taped to their hands: red in the palms and green on the backs of the fingers. So, as you were being brought forward, the plane handler had his palms closed and all you could see were the green lights on the outside of his closed fists. When he wanted you to stop, he'd just hold up both hands in the typical stop gesture and you would only see his red palm lights. But these were non-standard procedures and if you made a night landing aboard a carrier other than your own, you never knew what type of taxi or other signals you would receive.

'There was a lot of waiting and litle actual nighttime flying at that point. The Japanese had been pretty badly beaten during the Second Battle of the Philippine Sea and were apparently simply unable to commit the numbers of aircraft

to battle that they had in earlier battles. Consequently, our night fighter detachment aboard USS *Yorktown* flew on a fairly regular basis with the day fighters of VF-3. Actually, we *had* to fly with the day pilots just to maintain our proficiency. If you don't fly at least once or twice a week aboard a carrier, even during the day, you begin to lose your touch and would certainly be unable to continue participating in nighttime operations.

'To maintain proficiency with the F6F-5N and its APS-6B radar capability, we made mock attacks on other Navy aircraft during bad weather. Since you could only see the radar screen in reduced light, we put a blue hood over the scope whenever we flew daytime practice missions. We volunteered our services as daytime CAP pilots during cloudy weather, since we had radar and could follow an enemy aircraft into the clouds. That didn't work well, however, because chasing other airplanes inside clouds is a difficult job at best, due to the turbulence found in clouds. Trying to fly the airplane on instruments and use the radar to line up an evasive target while bouncing around inside a small thunderstorm was not my idea of having a good time.

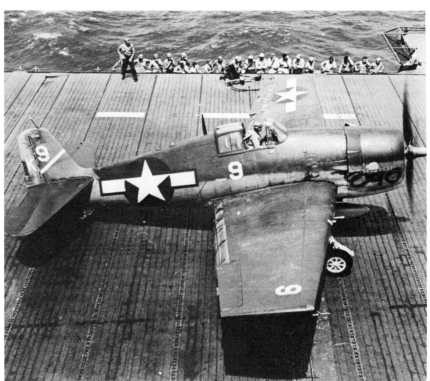

'However, we did have a useful role as strike leaders during bad weather. I led several of the strikes into Formosa and the northern Philippines in January of 1945. We always went in "under" the weather, which was typical heavy monsoon rain. The bottoms of the clouds were down to 1,500ft and we flew along at altitudes from 700 to 1,200ft. We were always concerned about running into a precipitous island such as Formosa, where the cliffs rise up 3,000 to 4,000ft. By flying out in front and using my radar, however, I could tell the rest of the formation our range and the location of the coast. Then we would all turn in time to proceed up the coast. Obviously, we couldn't attack what we couldn't see, but by getting close to our target this way, we usually managed to find a hole in the clouds that would give us a visual sighting of some enemy position. We attacked several enemy seaplane bases and other targets in northern Formosa using this technique.

'The APS-6 radar we used during World War 2 did not have a centre cursor with a sweep the way modern radar does. Rather, the presentation it offered was a series of small glowing images, which, with practice, could be identified as ships on water, aircraft in the air and various types of land mass formations. The object's relative location on the scope gave you some idea of where it was in relation to your aircraft; if it was

in the centre of the screen, it was in front of you, or you could judge how far to the left or right it was. If the "blip" was at the top of the scope, you knew it was 18 or 20 miles ahead of you.

'Our radar gear also had a gun-firing mode and when you switched to this mode, the outline of an airplane's wings appeared on your scope. Then you just kept approaching the target until the radar presentation of it filled that outline, which was when you were within range of it. At that point you opened fire. But that was a sticky business because you never actually saw your opponent and there was certainly a great danger that you could shoot down an American or Allied aircraft. We had received some training in trying to identify aircraft at night by their exhaust flare patterns, but that, too, was sticky business.

'When we did fly at night, we were usually

*Top left:* Three 'Betty' bombers come in low over the water as they attack US Navy ships in 1945. /US Navy

*Centre left:* F6F-5 Hellcat of VF-1 prepares for take-off. VF-1 succeeded VF-3 aboard USS *Yorktown* (CV-10) and remained with the ship until the Japanese surrender./US Navy

*Below left:* 'Top Hatters' of VF-1 are readied for take-off from USS *Yorktown* (CV-10). The squadron's well known insignia appears below the forward canopy. /US Navy

*Below:* While some members of the crew of USS *Yorktown* (CV-10) work on aircraft for the next day's air operations, other members (background) watch Hollywood films in one of the carrier's large hangar bays. /US Navy

*Right:* Curtiss SB2C Helldiver in the markings of Air Group 7 aboard USS *Hancock* (CV-19). /US Navy

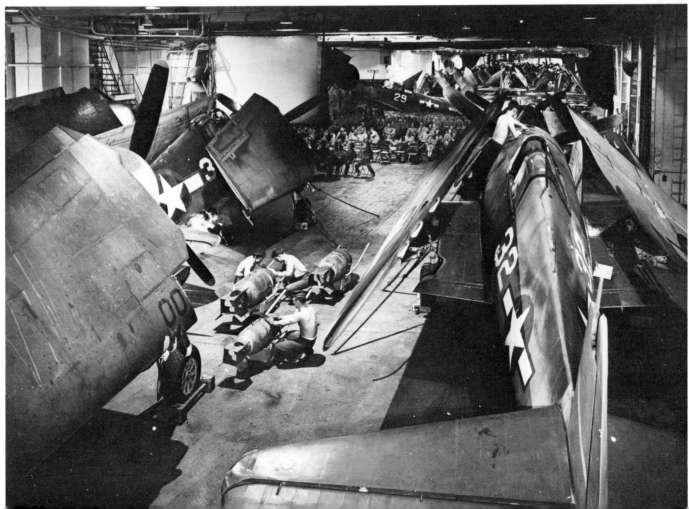

*Top:* Curtiss SB2C Helldiver in the markings of Air Group 1 aboard USS *Yorktown* (CV-10)./*US Navy*

*Above:* Curtiss SB2C Helldiver in the markings assigned on 27 July 1945 to all aircraft aboard USS *Shangri-La* (CV-38)./*US Navy*

launched with the last flight of the day and stayed out until all of that flight's aircraft were recovered. That way, if any Japanese aircraft did come out to attack the Fleet at sunset, we would be ready for them. Even after we were brought aboard, however, we remained on alert. While the rest of the ship's aircraft were made ready for the next day's morning strike, we were refueled and brought forward to each of the two forward catapults, port and starboard; one Hellcat was in position on each catapult and two others were spotted nearby for easy access to the catapult. All four night fighters had the engine starting units plugged in so we could go at a moment's notice. If there were no night bogies, we would be secured from that "Condition One Alert" –

actually being in the aircraft – at about 2200hrs and be sent to the squadron ready room, where we stayed up all night in a "Condition Two Alert", ready to launch within 15 minutes.

'One evening while on a "Condition One Alert", sitting in the cockpit of my Hellcat, I was startled to hear that a low-level attack by "Betty" bombers was coming in toward the *Yorktown*. Since they had come in very low and had evaded detection by our early warning system, it was too late to launch the night fighters. They would have to be taken under gunfire from the carrier. As the "Bettys" approached our bow, the ship's forward five-inch 38 guns were depressed to fire on the water – despite the fact that such gunfire would be directed right over our aircraft on and

near the catapult! Needless to say, to be almost right under the muzzles of such guns is deafening. Although neither my pilots nor I suffered any ill effects from this experience, four of our five Hellcats were total wrecks. The pressure waves from the guns caused tremendous rips in the skin of each aircraft; in fact, so much metal skin was blown out that it looked as though the four airplanes had had bombs go off in them. We eventually salvaged what we could from those airplanes and then pushed the remains over the side. Fortunately, there were some other night fighters in the Fleet and we managed to acquire three of them.'

After participating in the fierce carrier strikes on Tokyo and supporting the invasion of Iwo Jima, Air Group 3 left USS *Yorktown* in April 1945 and was succeeded by Air Group 1. George Cassell, then the senior night fighter pilot in Air Group 3, accepted the assignment of Executive Officer of VF-3. He went with the squadron to NAS Atlantic City, New Jersey, where the unit was re-formed with new aircraft and personnel to prepare for another combat tour that would have taken place if the war had continued into the autumn of 1945. He helped prepare the new VF-3 pilots for a role that underscored the rapid changes being made in nighttime operations.

'We would have gone back to the Pacific in October aboard either USS *Essex* or *Hancock*,' Adm Cassell recalls, 'But we would have been strictly a day unit and would have had no night fighter detachment. That responsibility would have been carried out by one of the night carriers that would have been in the Fleet by that time.'

Subsequent events proved the value of such concentrated night time flight operations, both

to hit enemy positions and to ward off any possible night attacks. During Adm Cassell's more than three decades of Navy service he saw the early F6F-5N night operations give way to the sophisticated carrier-based aircraft of today, which routinely operate during the day and at night.

One of the aircraft carriers that underwent that transition was USS *Yorktown*, which was decommissioned after World War 2 but brought back to Fleet service at the conclusion of the Korean Conflict in 1953. She saw service in the Pacific and the Atlantic until decommissioned again on 27 June 1970. USS *Yorktown* has since been acquired by the Patriot's Point American Naval and Maritime Museum in Charlestown, South Caroline, where the story of her long and varied service is preserved in a variety of artifacts and displays.

*Top:* USS *Hancock* (CV-19) underway in the South Pacific in 1944./*US Navy*

*Above:* Curtiss SB2C-4E (BuNo 20543) crashes following emergency landing aboard USS *Shangri-La* (CV-38) on 3 February 1945./*US Navy*

# Bad Day at Kure

Damage control teams fight fires
caused when a Kamikaze aircraft
hit the forward flight deck of USS
*Saratoga* (CV-3) on 21 February
1945./*US Navy*

*Above:* The first aircraft carrier USS *Hornet* (CV-8) at sea in 1941. /*US Navy*

The 'Essex' class carrier CV-12 was laid down as USS *Kearsarge* on 3 August 1942. The name honoured a famous Union warship from the American Civil War. However, after the first aircraft carrier named USS *Hornet* (CV-8) was sunk off Santa Cruz Island on 27 October 1942, CV-12 was quickly renamed to honour the memory of the ship that had launched Jimmy Doolittle's famed first American air raid on the Japanese homeland. The second carrier *Hornet* was christened on 30 August 1943 by the woman who had sponsored the first *Hornet* less than three years earlier, Mrs Frank Knox, wife of the Secretary of the Navy.

Entering the Pacific Theatre of Operations in the spring of 1944, the new *Hornet* quickly swung into action, launching aircraft for the 31 March strike against the Palau Islands. For the next several months *Hornet*-based aircraft continued to strike Japanese targets as American naval forces advanced ever westward. During the 'Marianas Turkey Shoot' in June, *Hornet* aircraft joined with those led by Cdr David McCampbell from USS *Essex* to inflict heavy losses on Japanese air units in the Philippine Sea. As a follow-up, on 20 June, *Hornet*'s aircraft attacked elements of the Japanese fleet at Rota and were given full credit for destroying the Japanese fleet carrier *Shokaku*.

USS *Hornet* enjoyed such success during the summer and autumn of 1944 that on 26 November 1944 the ship's Plan of the Day boastfully proclaimed:

'Today will be Field Day.[1] Air department dust off all overheads,[2] removing all snoopers[3] which may be adrift and sweep all corners of the Philippines, sending to the incinerator or throwing over the side (after first punching holes in the bottoms) any Nip cans,[4] APs[5] or AKs[6] still on topside.[7] Gunnery Department will assist as necessary. Engineering, continue to pour on the coal. Medics, stand by with heat rash lotion. Damage Control, observe holiday routine.[8]'

The boast was well deserved. *Hornet* launched strike after strike as the Allies pushed to retake the Philippines, the major southern base needed to reinforce attacks against Japan. The Alllies pushed farther into Japanese waters in late 1944 and early 1945 and, on 10 February, USS *Hornet* (CV-12) completed the mission begun by her illustrious predecessor some 34 months earlier. She launched air strikes against Tokyo in the first

[1]Navy slang for completely cleaning up an area.
[2]Slang for ceilings, in this case altitude ceilings.
[3]Slang for enemy intruders.
[4]Slang for Japanese destroyers.
[5]Navy designation for troop transport ships.
[6]Navy deignation for matériel transport ships.
[7]Slang for the surface, or above decks.
[8]Slang for a day of light duties and minimal efforts.

full-scale carrier attack on the Japanese homeland. The carrier operated 200 miles off Honshu and her aircraft were unchallenged as they pierced bad weather to hit the Japanese capital. Five days later *Hornet* returned to Japan as the US Navy began a regular routine of hitting targets in the home islands.

USS *Hornet* spent 10 days at Ulithi Atoll in March and then returned to Japanese waters as part of the naval force involved in the Battle for Okinawa. During this cruise the carrier had aboard one of the newly-constituted fighter bomber squadrons, VBF-17. On 2 January 1945, 18 of the VBF squadrons were commissioned within existing carrier air groups to give them greater diversity as needs shifted in the Pacific. While VF squadrons continued to perform the fighter mission and VB squadrons the carrier-based bomber mission, VBF units operated fighter aircraft that could swiftly deliver bombs and rockets, and *still* be effective as fighters. Hence, when Air Group 17 was sent out on 19 March to hit enemy shipping at anchor in Kure and Kobe naval bases, VBF-17 was assigned to be the advance element.

During strikes the previous day, Task Force 58 aircrews had reported sighting 16 important ships in the area, including the so-called super battleship *Yamato*, the battleship-carriers *Hyuga* and *Ise*, the fleet carriers *Amagi* and *Katsuragi*, and the light carrier *Ryuho*. But hitting these targets would be difficult because of the inland position of the bases, located on the main island of Honshu and effectively shielded from the Pacific by the large island of Shikoku. Further,

*Top:* The most memorable mission of USS *Hornet* (CV-8) was as the launching platform for the 18 April 1942 raid on Tokyo led by (then) Lt-Col Jimmy Doolittle in B-25 bombers./*US Navy*

*Above:* B-25 takes off down the flight deck of USS *Hornet* (CV-8) during start of Doolittle's raid on Tokyo./*US Navy*

*Right:* Japanese carrier-based torpedo aircraft makes a run on USS *Hornet* (CV-8) during the Battle of Santa Cruz. The carrier was sunk on 26 October 1942. /*US Navy*

*Below right:* Grumman F6F-3 Hellcats from VF-8 deployed aboard USS *Intrepid* (CV-11) after USS *Hornet* (CV-8) was sunk at Santa Cruz./*Grumman Aerospace*

*Above:* Curtiss SB2C Helldiver approaches the second carrier USS *Hornet* (CV-12) during operations in the South China Sea in 1945. On the flight deck aircraft are being moved forward while recovery operations are underway. */US Navy*

the large numbers of Navy aircraft assigned to attack those major targets left a severely reduced fighter cover available to defend the Task Force itself. As a consequence, land-based Japanese aircraft slipped through the CAP defence and struck the American carriers USS *Wasp* (CV-18) and *Franklin* (CV-13), setting off internal explosions in both ships. USS *Franklin* nearly sank and was effectively put out of action for the duration of the war.

The bad day for the carriers was matched by the devastation suffered by VBF-17, which lost one-third of its Grumman F6F-5 Hellcats during a massive engagement with fighters from the 343rd Kokutai (naval air group). Although the US Navy fighters shot down at least 24 of their opponents, the incident was recorded as 'the most determined and effective interception yet encountered by this Air Group.'

Lt E.S. Conant, Executive Officer of VBF-17, led the 20 Hellcats that were launched from USS *Hornet* beginning at 0618hrs. They were scheduled to rendezvous with 16 of Air Group 82's fighters from USS *Bennington* (CV-20) and

proceed on a fighter sweep against four airfields in the Kure area: Matsuyama West, Iwakuni, Hingahina and one at Kure itself. The combined fighter units were to destroy Japanese fighters in the target area prior to the arrival of the strike aircraft, which would be launched against the ships an hour later.

VBF-17 formed up into five divisions of four aircraft each:

| | |
|---|---|
| Lt E.S. Conant | Lt S.T. Kipp |
| Lt(jg) F.M. McCormick | Ens W.S. Matthews |
| Lt F.J. Prinz | Lt(jg) M.D. Harduff |
| Lt(jg) R.W. Karr | Ens E. Holley |
| | |
| Lt R. Moore | Lt(jg) C.T. Beall |
| Ens G. Edling | Ens R.O. Evans |
| Ens F.R. Chapman | Lt(jg) B.A. Eberts |
| Ens R. Grosso | Ens N.L. Hannah |
| | |
| Lt C.F. Weiss | |
| Ens A. Clark | |
| Lt R.L. Junghans | |
| Ens H. Yeremian | |

The ACA Report notes that:
'When the *Hornet* group reached the rendezvous point, the *Bennington* group had already gone, so the 20 VBF-17 planes set course for the target area. They passed over the western side of Shikoku and were approximately six miles northwest of that island, over Iyo-Nada, when some 40 fighters, mostly "Zekes", "Franks" and "Georges", were sighted ahead, flying at approximately 13,000ft on a southeasterly course.

'The *Hornet* planes were flying a northwesterly course at 12,000ft. The Jap planes were flying a right formation of four-plane divisions and two-plane sections. The divisions were strung out in line and stepped down slightly. As the two groups closed, the Jap planes passed into the overcast just above 13,000ft, with all but the two rear divisions disappearing into the clouds as they passed on the starboard beam and above.

'Lt Conant, watching the two divisions of Japs, which hung below the overcast, observed that the enemy group was starting a 180-degree turn to get to the rear of his formation. He immediately led his flight into a hard 180-degree turn also, in order to meet the Japs head-on. While the flight was in this turn, Lt Conant observed two enemy fighters dive out of the formation, apparently acting as decoys, while the balance of the flight climbed in the overcast. Just as the turn was completed, the enemy fighters were sighted approaching head-on, with altitude advantage. The *Hornet* group pulled up and attacked. Simultaneously, the Jap formation began taking offensive action, breaking off from above, making two-plane section attacks, recovering together, joining up, climbing to an altitude advantage of 1,000 to 1,500ft into the overcast and attacking again. From this point on the fight became a general melee which lasted from 0805 until 0830hrs.

*Below:* Grumman F6F-3 Hellcat of VF-11 has its wings folded by flight deck crewmen after landing aboard USS *Hornet* (CV-12) following raid over the Marianas./*US Navy*

'In the initial attack, a "Frank" made a run on Lt Conant's division from ahead and above. Conant turned head-on into him and fired into his engine from 2 o'clock, 20 degres below. When the range closed to approximately 200ft, Conant broke down and around to the left. The Jap pilot bailed out.

'Shortly thereafter, Conant saw an F6F, believed to be his wingman, Lt(jg) McCormick, diving down in front of him with a "Frank" on his tail, firing. He followed him down and made a highside [attack] on the Jap at 9 o'clock, firing a long burst into the port side of his fuselage from the cockpit forward. The "Frank" burst into flames over the entire forward end of the fuselage, and then exploded. By the time Conant recovered from this attack, he was down to 10,000ft and found himself bracketed by three more "Franks", one on either side and one above. He began "scissors" manoeuvres, which took him down to 3,000ft before he eventually got a snap burst into the port side of one of the Japs, who began smoking, rolled off to the left and dropped out of sight. After this Jap was "probable", the other two broke off their attack and Conant went back up to rejoin the melee going on at 12,000ft.

'In this initial attack by the "Franks", two members of this division dropped out of sight and were not seen again. Lt(jg) McCormick and Lt(jg) Karr are missing in action.* The fourth man in the division, Lt Prinz, was badly shot up in the first attack run. 20mm fire from an unidentified Jap fighter rendered his guns inoperative and shot out his hydraulic system. He returned to base alone and made a "no flap" landing aboard [the carrier]. The plane was surveyed [stricken from the operational list], but Lt Prinz was not injured.

'Lt Kipp's division was attacked by four fighters at the beginning of the fight. The division went into a weave and made a 180-degree turn. One "Frank" pulled out of his dive at the same level with Ens Matthews, Lt Kipp's wingman, and right in front of him. Matthews opened fire at the "Frank's" tail from close range and the plane exploded.

'While Matthews was attacking the "Frank", the division closed up, with Ens Holley weaving over the top of Kipp and Harduff. A "Zeke" made a pass at the division and dived through; Holley followed him down, firing into his tail. The 'Zeke" put his flaps down and levelled off at 8,000ft. Holley opened fire at 5 o'clock level from short range, the tracers entering the starboard wingroot. Flames enveloped the cockpit, the wingroots and cowling, and the plane crashed on the beach a few miles south of Matsuyama West airfield. Holley had started to climb back into the melee when a single 'Zeke"

*Lt(jg) Forrest E. McCormick in F6F-5 BuNo 71754 and Lt(jg) Roger W. Karr in F6F-5 BuNo 70675 were last seen heading down just over the inland sea, 10 miles northwest of Shikoku. Karr's aircraft was observed to be burning and out of control.

*Above left:* Grumman F6F-5 Hellcat revs up its engine prior to taking off from the starboard catapult aboard USS *Bennington* (CV-20). The catapult bridle can be seen linking the aircraft to the catapult./*US Navy*

*Left:* Although USS *Hornet* (CV-12) missed being hit by Kamikazes during operations off Kure, her sister ship, USS *Franklin* (CV-13) was not so lucky. That carrier was badly damaged, but managed to return to the United States as proof that no 'Essex' class carrier was ever sunk in battle./*US Navy*

*Above:* Captured Japanese aircraft at Atsugi Air Base in Japan. Various camouflage patterns can be seen./*US Air Force*

dove down and made a head-on approach, then pulled off to the left. Holley turned onto his tail and opened fire with a long burst. The plane flamed and crashed on the beach south of the above-named airfield.

'A little later, Lt(jg) Harduff, leader of the second section, saw a "Frank" start a run on Lt Kipp. Harduff's section was weaving on the port beam of Kipp. As the "Frank" came down on Kipp's tail, Harduff pulled around onto him and opened fire from 300ft and 20 degrees below into the Jap's engine and cowling. The "Frank" broke off his run, rolled to the left and exploded. During the entire melee, Lt(jg) Harduff smoked five other Jap fighters: two "Franks" and three "Zekes". These planes were smoking to such an extent that they are being carried as probably destroyed.

'Twice during the melee, Lt Kipp destroyed a "Frank" on the tail of his second section. On both occasions the "Frank" was attacking from above and behind Lt(jg) Harduff and Ens Holley, the second section. Both times Kipp was on the starboard side of his weave, pulled up, went across the top of the section and fired long bursts into the "Frank's" engines as they made their attack runs. One plane flamed all over and the other exploded.

'Approximately ten minutes before the end of the melee, a "Frank" dived right through Lt Kipp's division. Ens Matthews tagged onto his tail and opened fire. He dove down toward the water with him. The "Frank" was flamed before he hit the bay. This was the last time Ens Matthews was seen. [Ens Edwin W. Matthews in F6F-5 BuNo 79910 was last seen diving on the enemy fighter.]

'Right at the end of the fight, Lt Kipp's division, minus Ens Matthews, was about to leave the area en route to base when it was attacked by four "Zekes". This division and approximately two more were all that were left at

the scene of the engagement. The *Hornet* division was at 9,000ft and the Japs began diving down from above, two planes at a time, attacking on both sides simultaneously. One "Zeke" came down tail-on between Lt Kipp and Lt(jg) Harduff. The divison was weaving, but a 20-mm burst hit Kipp's starboard wing, which started trailing fire from the hole. Ens Holley was above and to the right of the section. He turned into the attacking plane and fired a full deflection shot at the "Zeke" making the run on Kipp. The Jap pulled off to the left, losing altitude, flaming in the cowling and wingroots and trailing volumes of smoke. Holley and Harduff joined up on Kipp and headed southwest across Shikoku for the sea. Kipp's plane was still burning in the starboard wing, but he was able to fly straight and level at 200kt. Suddenly, however, his starboard wing broke off, the fuselage broke in two, just aft of the cockpit, and he crashed in flames five miles southwest of Matsuyama West airfield. [Lt Strother T. Kipp in F6F-5 BuNo 70859 was listed as missing in action.]

'Lt Moore's division destroyed five Jap planes in the fight. Near the start of the melee, Lt Moore saw a "Zeke" chasing an F6F, approximately 1,000ft below and on a crossing course. Moore started for him, made an overhead run, opened fire at 800ft and saw tracers entering the cockpit of the "Zeke". The cockpit flamed and the "Zeke" rolled over out of control.

'During this attack by Lt Moore, his wingman, Ens Edling, shot down a Jap. When Moore started for the "Zeke" above, Edling followed close on Moore's tail. Suddenly, two "Georges" dived between Moore and Edling, and Edling flipped up to his left and apparently the "George" did the same thing, bcause he [Edling] found himself on the "George's" tail at 4 o'clock. He opened fire at 900ft and saw tracers entering the tail. The plane did not burn. He pulled up his lead and put bursts into the cockpit. The plane flipped over to the left and went down. Edling observed it crash in the water.

'After shooting down this plane, Edling could not locate his division again. When he was about to set course for base, he was attacked by a plane that made a 90-degree deflection run on him. He tried to turn in to his attacker, but found that his elevator control was gone. The enemy plane did not press his attack. On the way back to base, flying on [trim] tab [in place of the malfunctioning elevator], a "George" started chasing him, but by putting everything forward and climbing 4,000ft at 200kts he was able to lose the "George".

'About 10 minutes after he shot down the "Zeke", Lt Moore tailed in on a "George" and made a run at 5 o'clock from 200ft range. He saw his tracers hitting the fuselage and starboard wing. A six-inch-diameter fire started in the wingroot, and small pieces were seen flying off the plane. The "George" then pulled off to the right and started down. Moore did not follow. Just then he was hit in the engine by fire from a plane he did not see, which sprayed oil all over his windshield and started a bad engine vibration. En route home he was attacked twice. One plane knocked him into a spin with a tail attack. He recovered at 9,000ft. Over Shikoku, another plane attacked him, peppering his wings and starting a fire in his starboard wing, which later went out. Lt Moore had just come within sight of the Task Force screen when his engine started losing power and he was forced to make a water landing ahead of the screen. [Lt Moore ditched in F6F-5 BuNo 72913.] He sustained a sprained ankle when he made a no-flap landing in the water. He was rescued 15 minutes later by the [destroyer] USS *McKee* (DD-575).

'During the melee, Ens Chapman shot down two "Tonys". On both attacks he tailed in on the Japs, opened fire at 6 o'clock level, and observed the planes flame and crash into the bay. Ens Gross shot down two "Tonys". One he flamed in the engine from above, the other he fired long bursts into from behind; the second plane crashed on the west shore of Shikoku.

'Lt Weiss's division accounted for four Jap planes destroyed. Ens Yeremian attacked a "Zeke", which had just made a pass at another divison close by. He dropped on him from above and ahead, firing into his wingroots. [The "Zeke"] went down completely covered in flames. Later in the fight, Ens Yeremian tailed in on another "Zeke", flamed him at 5 o'clock and watched him crash into the water. This pilot [Yeremian] also attacked a third "Zeke", which dropped out of sight, smoking.

'During the melee, Ens Clark destroyed a "George" in an attack tail-on [from behind]. The plane burned and went down. [Clark] later destroyed a "Zeke" in a 90-degree deflection shot which tore out the canopy above the pilot's head. The [enemy] plane rolled over and dived in an inverted position into the sea. Lt Weiss, leader of this division, disappeared during the melee and did not return to base. [Lt Charles F. Weiss in F6F BuNo 72372 was last seen in the midst of the aerial combat and was subsequently listed as missing in action.]

'Lt(jg) Beall's division shot down five planes in the fight. The division was in a weave position when a "Zeke" got on Beall's tail. Ens Evans pulled up, firing a full deflection shot, and the "Zeke" pulled up and went down. Beall saw him splash into the water. Lt(jg) Beall shot down a "George", which dived out of the overcast on to the division. He got on the Jap's tail and fired a four-second burst which flamed the fuselage behind the cockpit. The "George" crashed into the water.

'Lt(jg) Eberts accounted for two "Georges" and one "Tony" during this engagement. He shot down the first "George" in a head-on run. The engine smoked and [the "George"] crashed into the water. The second "George" and the "Tony" were found by Eberts on the tails of F6Fs. In both cases [Eberts] made tail approaches, chased the Japs down to the deck, firing on the way, and saw them crash on the land near Maysayama West airfield.

'It was the opinion of the more experienced pilots of this squadron who participated in this melee that the Jap pilots encountered here were superior to those met in the Tokyo area [during USS *Hornet*'s February raid]. They handled their planes well, were exceedingly aggressive, and exhibited good organisation, discipline and tactics. Their tactics were similar to those of the US Navy. They appeared to be well trained and experienced in combat flying.'

In addition to expressing the pilots' regard for their adversaries, as a final note, the VBF-17 ACA Report compared the Japanese 'Tony' and 'George' fighters to the squadron's Hellcats:
' "Tony" vs Hellcat: At 10,000ft, "Tony" in a tight flipper turn could not turn inside an F6F [that was] using full throttle and [attaining] 2,400rpm in a dive. One pilot, indicating 420kts, caught a "Tony". "Tony" will not burn easily.

' "George" vs Hellcat: One pilot reported that, at altitudes around 10,000ft, an F6F using full throttle and [attaining] 2,300rpm, without use of water injection, easily caught a "George" in a dive.'

Of the 20 VBF-17 aircraft assigned to attack Kure, five crashed over Japanese territory, leaving their pilots to an uncertain fate. One Hellcat ditched within sight of Task Force 58 and one barely made it back to USS *Hornet*, where it was stricken from the operational rolls. Two other Hellcats – BuNos 71781 and 72676 – were so badly damaged during the aerial combat that they were also surveyed after returning to the carrier.

On the positive side, however, VBF-17 pilots accounted for 24 confirmed 'kills' among their

*Left:* Kawanishi H6K5 Navy Type 97 flying boat ('Mavis') going down in flames after being fired on by US Navy aircraft over the Pacific. /*US Navy*

*Below left:* Hellcats of Air Group 12 aboard USS *Randolph* (CV-15) ride out rough weather prior to the invasion of Iwo Jima./*US Navy*

*Below:* While one VF-12 Hellcat sits on the port catapult of USS *Randolph* (CV-15), another moves up to the starboard 'cat' which has just launched the aircraft seen rotating off the bow (turning off the centre-line of the carrier). /*US Navy*

adversaries and were credited with 'probable' victories over an additional six Japanese fighters. While 19 March 1945 was a bad day for VBF-17 and for Task Force 58, it was without doubt an even worse day for the Japanese naval fighters of the 343rd Kokutai and other units that attempted to intercept the *Hornet*-based Hellcats.

Air Group 17 remained involved in operations supporting the invasion of Okinawa and attacks on the home islands of Japan. On 7 April, aircraft from USS *Hornet* participated in the sinking of the battleship *Yamato* and, nine days later, during a fierce attack by Japanese suicide aircraft, Air Group 17 fighters shot down 54 aircraft during the day-long engagement.

USS *Hornet* (CV-12) remained in the forward combat zone during the early summer of 1945 and only the forces of nature denied the carrier a role in the final assault that led to victory over the Japanese. The ship rode out a typhoon that began on 3 June, but a giant wave on the morning of 5 June collapsed the forward part of *Hornet*'s flight deck and put the carrier out of action for the duration of the hostilities. She returned to the western Pacific in September 1945 as part of the 'Magic Carpet Fleet' of ships used to transport veterans home from the former battlefields.

*Above:* Curtiss SB2C Helldiver of VB-17 swerves on landing aboard USS *Bunker Hill* (CV-17) on 11 September 1943./*US Navy*

*Left:* Smoke pours from aft flight deck of USS *Bunker Hill* (CV-17) after the ship was hit by two Kamikazes within 30 minutes on 11 May 1945./*US Navy*

# Intrepid Indeed

During the Tripolitan War, 24-year old Lt Stephan Decatur, Jr sailed the first USS *Intrepid* into Tripoli Harbour and, on the night of 16 February 1804, led his men on a lightning-swift raid that destroyed the captured American vessel *Philadelphia* right in the midst of the enemy's defences. Lord Nelson called *Intrepid*'s mission 'the most bold and daring act of the age'.

A little more than 140 years later, a namesake of that vessel, the aircraft carrier USS *Intrepid* (CV-11), sailed into the combat zone in the Pacific and sustained some of the heaviest battle damage inflicted during World War 2. Her several trips to the repair yards earned *Intrepid* the unflattering sobriquet 'The Hardluck I', Yet, even in the face of determined attacks by Japanese suicide aircraft, *Intrepid* and her air groups kept coming back. The ship was aptly named.

*Intrepid* was the fifth of the 24 'Essex' class aircraft carriers placed in commission. Her keel was laid down at the Newport News Shipbuilding Company in Virginia on 1 December 1941, six days before the Japanese attack on Pearl Harbor that brought America into the war, and the carrier was completed and christened 17 months later, on 26 April 1943.

*Intrepid*'s first commanding officer was Capt Thomas L. Sprague, a US Naval Academy graduate who had been a naval aviator since 1921. He took *Intrepid* out for a Caribbean shakedown cruise in October and, a month later, was ordered to head for the Pacific with Air Group 8 aboard. While passing through the Panama Canal with a canal pilot at the helm, the new carrier went aground and sustained minor damage. Thus, once on the Pacific side of the canal, *Intrepid* headed for the Hunter's Point naval shipyard in California for the first of several wartime repair periods.

On 6 January 1944, Air Group 6, previously aboard USS *Enterprise* (CV-6), reported aboard *Intrepid*. Ten days later they were en route to the combat zone to take part in Operation 'Flintlock', the invasion of Majuro, a key point in the Marshall Islands. Air Group 6 began with a series of attacks on small islands in the Kwajalein chain on 29 January. VB-6's Douglas SBD-5 Dauntlesses rolled in with 500lb bombs, as VT-6's Grumman TBF Avengers delivered 2,000lb bombs against major enemy airfield targets. All the while, VF-6's Grumman F6F-3 Hellcats flew CAP missions, which, by 7 February, resulted in seven enemy aircraft shot out of the air and another 17 destroyed on the ground.

A week later came the attack on Truk, preparatory to the invasion of Eniwetok, another major atoll in the Marshall Islands. *Intrepid*-based aircraft were joined by aircraft of Air Group 9 from USS *Essex* (CV-9) and Air Group 31 from the light carrier USS *Cabot* (CVL-28). The large force anticipated meeting most of the 365 Japanese aircraft known to be based at Truk. Although some 40 enemy aircraft had departed Truk the night before the American raid, the aircraft from Task Group 58.2 were greeted by 45 defenders.

Lt Alexander Vraciu, Jr, a pilot from VF-6 aboard *Intrepid* who went on to become a 19-victory ace, described the action in his ACA report:

'We noticed that the Jap pilots weren't reluctant to attack, but once they were cornered, they'd dive steeply for the water or cloud cover, The Hellcat can definitely out-manoeuvre the "Zero" at speeds of 250kts and better, so we began to follow them down. I was able to follow three planes down in this manner, two being "Zeros" and one a "Rufe", and set them afire. All hit the water inside Truk Atoll. While climbing back up for altitude after one of the above [noted] attacks, I noticed a "Zero" skirting a not-too-thick cloud, so I made a pass at him, but he promptly headed for a thicker one. After playing cat and mouse with him for some minutes, I climbed into the sun and let him think I had retired. When I came down on him for the last time, from 5 o'clock above, he never knew what hit him, I'm sure. His wing tank and cockpit exploded.'

With 30 of the defending Japanese aircraft put out of action, the fighters from the three carriers then turned their attention to enemy aircraft on the ground at Moen, Eten and Param fields. Despite heavy enemy anti-aircraft fire, the combined Navy fighter force destroyed another 40 aircraft. *Intrepid*'s fighters accounted for 15 'Bettys', eight 'Zekes' and one unidentified type.

Two days later, however, enemy gunners took their toll, as noted in VF-6's ACA report for 16 February:

'Lt G.C. Bullard, Executive Officer of VF-6, did an outstanding job of strafing from low altitude, making at least 12 runs up and down [the] Moen bomber strip. En route to the rendezvous point, he spotted a "Katori" class cruiser heading north in the lagoon between North East and North Passes, and led his division in a strafing attack down to low altitude. This [action] resulted in his being shot down by anti-aircraft fire. He made a water landing outside the lagoon, west of North Pass, within seven miles of three [Japanese destroyers] DDs; the DDs apparently waiting to rendezvous with an "Atago" class cruiser approaching from the east of North Pass.

'Lt(jg) Odenbrett followed him down and dropped a life raft, and, noting heavy AA around him, strafed the CA before leaving the locality, setting fire to the VOS [float plane] on the [cruiser's] catapult.

'It is hoped that Lt Bullard is now rescued, as he was last sighted by Lt-Cdr H.W. Harrison [the squadron commander], who observed that he had spelled out his name in rocks on the beach and was waving. The second time [he was spotted] food and water were dropped by a TBF. Commander Task Force 58.2 was notified and arrangements made for rescue the following day.'

The raid on Truk, a harbour much used by the enemy's Combined Fleet, has been somewhat idealistically called 'the Japanese Pearl Harbor'.

*Left:* Curtiss SB2C Helldivers of VB-10 pass USS *Intrepid* (CV-11) during late afternoon mission. */US Navy*

While it may not have had quite the chilling effect that the Japanese raid on 7 December 1941 had on American forces, the Truk raid was certainly quite successful and cost the Japanese considerable tonnage. Air Group 6 alone flew 192 combat sorties, eight CAPs and 10 Anti-Submarine Patrols (ASPs), and inflicted heavy losses on the Japanese. A VB-6 Douglas Dauntless put a 1,000lb Semi-Armour Piercing bomb into an enemy cargo ship and practically blew it out of the water. Two other SBDs crippled a 'Katori' class light cruiser, which suffered further when the TBFs went after it and which was finally sunk by the heavy guns of American batleships lurking outside the lagoon. VF-6's Hellcats shot down 16 Japanese aircraft demolished 37 others on the ground.

It was a good day's work, complicated only by the late evening appearance of an unidentified aircraft on Intrepid's radar. Designated 'Raid Easy' by the ship's Combat Information Centre, the lone aircraft (presumed to be an enemy) first showed up at 2349hrs on 16 February. A night fighter from USS Yorktown (CV-10) was vectored to intercept the 'bogey', but the VF-5 Hellcat lost the contact at midnight. Intrepid was then ordered into a series of evasive manoeuvres, but 11 minutes later the carrier was struck by a torpedo released when 'Raid Easy' was 300yd abeam of the ship, flying at about 50ft

altitude. The marauder passed forward of the carrier to port and then was lost in the darkness.

The torpedo's explosion caused Intrepid to lurch violently to port and then to starboard. Two SBDs parked aft on the flightdeck were hurled over the fantail, and two of the ship's 20mm gun mounts were blown away, along with the aft starboard catwalk. The explosion killed 11 men and wounded 17 others.

Damage control parties were quickly mobilised to deal with the destruction, but the situation on Intrepid's bridge was hair-raising. The carrier was using 15 degrees left rudder when passing 180 degrees as part of a previously ordered turn the entire Task Group was making. Thus, Intrepid's rudder jammed in precisely that position and, instead of recovering from the turn, the carrier continued to turn slowly to port, nearly slicing the cruiser USS Wichita (CA-45) as that ship slipped just under the carrier's bow on the starboard side.

Eventually, Intrepid was brought on a steady course by using the ship's engines to steer. Full power was given to the port screws and one-third power to the starboard screws, thereby enabling the carrier to make a good course at about 22kts.

At 0144hrs on 17 February, Intrepid was detached from Task Group 58.2 and sent back to Eniwetok in the company of four destroyers, two cruisers and the light carrier USS Cabot. The

*Above:*USS *Intrepid* (CV-11) underway in the Pacific. /*via Pete Clayton*

*Top right:* F6F Hellcat landing aboard USS *Intrepid* (CV-11) in 1944./*US Navy*

*Right:* F6F Hellcats of VF-8 taxi down the flight deck of USS *Intrepid* (CV-11) as the carrier heads for the Pacific. /*Grumman Aerospace*

passage was relatively smooth until winds increased to 20-30kts off the port bow. At that point the carrier became completely unmanageable, as the forces of nature overcame the small measure of control that had been afforded by the varying engine power applied to the port and starboard screws. The main contributor to the loss of control was the carrier's 'island' superstructure above the flight deck, which acted like a huge sail in the wind. Capt Sprague likened *Intrepid* to 'a giant pendulum, swinging back and forth. She had a tendency to weathercock into the wind . . . [pointing] her bow toward Tokyo, but right then I wasn't interested in going in that direction.'

To reduce the weathercocking caused by the sail-like qualities of the 'island', it was decided to use the standard sailing ship remedy: increase the headsail. This was done by shifting most of the carrier's cargo weight aft, thereby bringing the ship's bow further out of the water and presenting it to the wind. While the cargo weight was being moved, all available aircraft from Air Group 6 were re-spotted on the forward end of the flight deck to give added surface area acting as the headsail. Then the outboard starboard driveshaft from the ship's engines was locked, while the port screws (on the side of the ship *opposite* to the 'island') continued to operate at full speed. That combination of screws and wind resistance allowed *Intrepid* to maintain a fairly steady course for about a day.

On the morning of 18 February 1944, it became apparent that additional measures would have to be taken to reduce the strain on the screws. To provide the necessary further wind resistance, a 'sail' was improvised from cargo nets, hatch covers, canvas and any other available materials. This 3,000sq ft of material was used to form a cover from the leading edge of the flight deck to the open forecastle, which extended forward of the flight deck. In this condition the damaged carrier managed to make a fairly steady 18kt course back to Oahu, Hawaii.

*Intrepid*'s still slightly erratic course caused Capt Sprague to quip: 'No enemy sub could have figured out her zig-zag plan. As a matter of fact, there was no plan; the pattern was created as we went along, and no one knew for sure how long she'd keep on anything like a straight course.'

*Intrepid* arrived at Pearl Harbor on 24 February. After emergency repairs were completed and she was deemed at least temporarly seaworthy, she returned to the United States. *Intrepid* went into the Hunter's Point drydock on 22 March and remained out of service until she completed post-repair sea trials on 3 June. Later that month, while transporting Air Group 8 to Hawaii, trouble with the ship's reduction gears postponed a planned combat deployment. Once again, temporary repairs were ordered and *Intrepid* was able to put to sea long enough to transport Air Group 19, led by Cdr Karl E. Jung, to the naval air station at Eniwetok.

Final repairs to the ship's reduction gears were completed in July and on 16 August 1944, the first anniversary of the ship's commissioning, *Intrepid* departed Pearl Harbor. As she headed out to sea, Cdr William E. Ellis led Air Group 18 aboard for the deployment. Cdr Ellis and the squadrons under his command swung into action

*Below: Intrepid*-based F4U Corsair fires rockets into Japanese island position./*US Navy*

on 6 September, flying aerial cover missions for the capture and occupation of the Southern Palau Islands. Two days later they hit Mindinao Island in the Philippines.

In the usual manner of the fast carrier attack groups, *Intrepid* made a high speed run into the launch point and then retreated from the area after the strike aircraft were recovered. That method of operation minimised the danger of the ship being hit by enemy aircraft and maximised the destructive range of Air Group 18's strike aircraft. During these hit-and-run attacks on Mindinao on 9 and 10 September, *Intrepid*'s aircraft destroyed a number of enemy aircraft on the ground at Davao Gulf and Matina. They went into the Visayan Sea area, well within the Philippine Islands themselves, to hit targets on 12, 13 and 14 September.

Some of the fierce air action is described in a VF-18 ACA report for the morning of 13 September. On that occasion, eight Grumman F6F-3 Hellcats from the fighter squadron were sent out to escort 12 Curtiss SB2C Helldivers from VB-18 armed with one 1,000lb and two 250lb bombs apiece, and 6 TBM-1C Avengers from VT-18 carrying four 500lb bombs apiece. Two of the eight Hellcats had also been assigned photo reconnaissance duties during this strike on Japanese airfields on the northern part of Negros Island. The ACA report notes:

'Lt C.E. Harris observed a "Zeke" making a pass at the formation from 6 o'clock below. His division dove on the attacker, causing it to break off and dive into the clouds below. The Hellcats broke out under the cloud base, where they observed 10 to 15 enemy fighters milling about.

They continued their dive, making a pass at the enemy aircraft, but their great surplus of speed caused them to overshoot. As the division pulled out of its dive at approximately 500ft, there were enemy fighters all about and a general melee resulted directly over Fabrica air strip at about 2,500ft. Lt(jg) F.N. Burley got on a "Zeke's" tail and soon had a "Zeke" on his own. Harris, about 1,000ft behind, turned inside and got a 30-degree deflection shot into the "Zeke", which burned instantly and exploded before hitting the ground. Just prior to this, Burley had gotten a burst into his "Zeke", but could not observe the result, as he turned sharply to the left to avoid the "Zeke" which was to be shot down by Harris a split second later.

'Harris started climbing back to the formation when at 5,000ft he observed a "Hamp" also climbing. Harris continued to 7,000ft, getting above the "Hamp", which made a slight turn back toward the airstrip. As he did so, Harris turned inside, got on his tail and shot him down in flames.

'Harris looked around for the other planes in his division (his receiver was out) and observed a melee at 7,000ft directly over the airstrip. As he headed for it, two "Hamps" came from above at 7 o'clock. Harris was making 150kts. He pulled straight up about 300ft [and] turned sharply above the "Hamps", which had continued their dive after making their pass, firing 20mm in short bursts. Harris pushed over into a 30-degree dive and easily overhauled the "Hamps", which began to separate as he fired a long burst into one. The "Hamp" exploded as it started a roll, [and] Harris again commenced to climb to try to

*Below:* Japanese 'Tony' fighter of the type shot down by *Intrepid* gunners during a Kamikaze attack. /*US Air Force*

121

find his group. He observed eight planes at 9 o'clock and made a climbing left turn toward them before identifying them as "Hamps". Using full rpm, full throttle, low blower and water injection, he pulled away from them easily. When 1,000ft above and 1,500 to 2,000ft ahead of the pursuing "Hamps", he decided to make a low side, forward of the beam run on them. They were in a wide formation and seemed to be firing single rounds with their 20mm guns but the range was too great for them to obtain hits. Harris pulled around sharply and made a low side run on the last one in the formation. The Jap appeared not to know what to do. Fire was opened at 700ft and the "Hamp" exploded when 200ft away. Harris nosed over, saw some Hellcats below headed for the rendezvous point and joined up with them. On the way back, the other members of the division joined up and a running rendezvous was made on departure for base.'

Further attacks on Japanese positions – especially airfields – in the Philippines were carried out in September. Following a brief replenishment at Ulithi Atoll, *Intrepid* turned her Air Group toward Okinawa and the Ryukyu Islands beginning on 10 October. Continuing the fast carrier attack group tactics, *Intrepid* turned two days later to Formosa, where her aircraft struck an enemy airfield at Shinchiku and a seaplane base at Tansui.

All throughout the battles off the Philippines that ran like a skein of destruction during the month of October, *Intrepid* successfully fended off land-based Japanese aircraft that had been sent out to attack her. But on 29 October 1944, a new form of aerial attack was encountered: the Kamikaze.

While Air Group 18's aircraft were busy hitting targets on Luzon, a large group of enemy aircraft was detected by radar at some 80 miles from the ship. All hands manned their battle stations as *Intrepid* went to General Quarters (GQ). The ship's gun mounts began firing at a lone 'Jill' attack bomber at about 1200hrs and,

*Below:* Formation of 'Betty' bombers flying out to attack US carrier force off the home islands of Japan./via R. Mikesh

having hit the aircraft as it approached the carrier, the gunners were then shocked to see the pilot make an obvious suicide dive for *Intrepid*. The Japanese aircraft missed the flight deck, but did hit a 20mm gun mount just below the flight deck on the starboard side. The gunners had remained at their battle station to the last and, in the ensuing crash and inferno of blazing gasoline, nine of them were burned to death.

To the western mind there was no understanding that, deprived of its once large aircraft carrier fleet, the Imperial Japanese Navy would commit some of its finest pilots and aircraft to missions of self destruction. Highly motivated by the centuries old code of Bushido, by which the legendary Samurai warriors had lived and died, volunteers proudly and eagerly applied for the Japanese Naval Special Attack Force. It has become better known as the Kamikaze (divine wind) Corps, named for the fortuitous wind storm that saved Japan from the Mongol Fleet in 1281, and is vividly remembered for the zeal of its members, who gave their best effort in attempting to halt the Allied advance toward the home islands of Japan.

The 29 October attack had been launched by elements of the 201st Kokutai (Naval Air Group) based at Nichols Field and, although that mission failed to inflict serious damage on USS *Intrepid*, subsequent missions caused severe damage to other American aircraft carriers and other ships.

Following the initial Kamikaze attack, *Intrepid* enjoyed a brief respite at Ulithi and then, on 19 November, launched strikes against enemy air installations at Nielson, Nichols and Clark airfields on Luzon. Ironically, the latter two facilities served as home bases for the Japanese Naval Special Attack Force. On 25 November, while Air Group 18 was attacking Luzon, Japanese suicide aircraft were once again directed toward the aircraft carriers that had launched the strike. At 1218hrs two 'Vals' made suicide dives on USS *Hancock* (CV-19) and USS *Cabot*. Both Kamikaze aircraft were splashed by a combination of the ships' CAP fighters and gunners. No further enemy aircraft were spotted until 1252hrs, when two 'Zekes' were observed eight miles out from *Intrepid*, approaching the carrier's stern from about 8,000ft. To complicate matters, Air Group 18 aircraft were orbiting the carrier preparatory to landing after completing their missions over Luzon. Most were recovered before the aft gun batteries opened up on the 'Zekes', one of which was hit just 1,500yd astern of the carrier.

A brief cease fire was ordered to avoid hitting *Intrepid*-based aircraft still orbiting astern of the ship. That event and the diversion created by yet another 'Zeke' off the carrier's starboard side, allowed the second of the two 'Zekes' astern to close in on *Intrepid*. The carrier's aft 20mm and 40mm gun mounts sent up a wall of fire to stop the 'Zeke' and did succeed in setting fire to it. But then the Kamikaze went into a power stall about 1,000yd astern of *Intrepid*, did a wingover

*Above:* Curtiss SB2C Helldiver in the markings of Air Group 8 aboard USS *Bunker Hill* (CV-17). /*US Navy*

*Left:* Mitsubishi G4M1 ('Betty') in green cross markings used to transport Japanese envoys to surrender ceremonies in 1945. /*US Navy*

*Above:* Japanese suicide aircraft hits the flight deck of USS *Intrepid* (CV-11) and spills over into the starboard catwalk./*US Navy*

at about 500ft and roared into the ship's flight deck. The bomb attached to the 'Zeke' pierced the flight deck and exploded in Squadron Ready Room 4, which was just below the flight deck. Fortunately, that compartment was empty at the time, but 32 men in an adjoining compartment were killed by the explosion.

The stricken carrier was immediately put into a hard right turn to allow the water and flaming gasoline in the hangar bay and on the flight deck to spill out over the port side of the ship, away from the critical control areas in the 'island' superstructure on the starboard side.

*Intrepid*'s uncharacteristically hard turn and the flames from the bomb's explosion alerted other Kamikaze aircraft in the same manner that a stricken or injured swimmer attracts the attention of sharks. Consequently, another 'Zeke' made a run on *Intrepid*'s starboard side. It was brought down by the combined fire power of several American ships near the carrier. But the smokey haze drifting across the carrier's flight deck obscured the vision of topside gunners, who missed the 'Zeke' coming in on *Intrepid*'s port quarter. He, too, was finally hit, but not before he went into a power stall and managed to aim for the forward portion of the flight deck. The bomb penetrated the flight deck and exploded in the forward hangar bay, where a number of aircraft were being overhauled. All available sailors rushed to join the damage control parties engaged in trying to contain the holocaust that had been set off. It took nearly three hours to snuff out the various fires and ventilate the hangar bay. At that time it was clear that 'The Hardluck I' had just earned another trip to the repair yard.

Moreover, there was now no doubt about the mission of the ship's adversaries. Cdr William E. Ellis, Commander of Air Group 18, summarised: 'Up to that time I had seen nothing to prove that these attacks were being carried out by suicide pilots. Even the first one that day appeared to me to be a dead pilot who just happened to crash on the ship. But after witnessing the second one climb, wing over and dive into us, I was convinced and became a believer.'

*Intrepid* withdrew from the battle line and returned to Ulithi, arriving there on 29 November. Two days later Air Group 18 was officially detached from the carrier in order to rebuild for the next combat cruise aboard a different ship. While operating aboard *Intrepid*, Air Group 18 had lost 66 of its own airplanes, as well as 31 pilots and 27 aircrewmen. On the plus side, Air Group 18 accounted for 154 enemy aircraft shot down, 240 damaged and 169 destroyed on the ground. Air Group 18 definitely sank 53 enemy ships, probably sank 30 more and damaged 135 vessels.

After a brief stay at Ulithi, *Intrepid* sailed back to Hawaii and thence to Hunter's Point, where the shipyard repair crews were beginning to take a proprietary interest in the carrier. This repair trip lasted until 11 February 1945, when *Intrepid* left Hunter's Point for post repair trials. The carrier passed all tests and, on 16 February, received a new complement of aircraft and crews.

*Intrepid*'s next wartime deployment was to be with Air Group 10 under the command of Cdr John J. Hyland. In anticipation of further Kamikaze attacks, Air Group 10 had a far greater number of fighter aircraft assigned to it than had any previous Air Group to deploy aboard *Intrepid*. Indeed, there was an additional squadron composed entirely of Vought F4U Corsairs, a powerful and manoeuvrable fighter once thought unsuitable for carrier use. Subsequent events proved the Corsair to be a formidable ship-based fighter.

Thus, Air Group 10 put to sea aboard *Intrepid* with 29 Vought F4U-1D Corsairs, one Goodyear-built FG-1 Corsair, four Grumman F6F-5N night-fighting Hellcats, and two Grumman F6F-5P photo-reconnaissance Hellcats, all part of VF-10 under the command of Lt-Cdr W.E. Clarke; 36 F4U-1Ds of VBF-10 commanded by Lt-Cdr W.E. Rawie; 15 Curtiss SB2C-4E Helldivers of VB-10 commanded by Lt-Cdr R.B. Buchan; and 15 TBM-3 Avengers of VT-10 commanded by Lt-Cdr J.C. Lawrence (who, incidentally, became Commanding Officer of USS *Intrepid* in 1963).

On March 1945, Air Group 10 launched its first strike from *Intrepid*. As part of Operation 'Iceberg' to secure a forward American base in the Ryukyu Islands, Air Group 10 joined other elements of Task Force 58 in attacking island-based aviation facilities still in Japanese hands. While that attack was in progress, however, Kamikaze aircraft from Kokubu went out after *Intrepid* and USS *Yorktown* (CV-10). Shortly

after 0800hrs, a twin-engine 'Frances' bomber approached the two carriers, zig-zagging and finally heading for *Intrepid*. Gunners aboard both carriers opened fire on the suicide plane, which crashed in the water just off *Intrepid*'s port bow.

A few minutes later, a 'Betty' made a shallow glide at 400-500ft altitude toward *Intrepid*. It, too, was hit, but fell so close to the carrier – within 100ft of it – that flaming gasoline and fragments hit *Intrepid*'s hangar deck and set off several small fires in Hangar Bay 1 (forward).

On 21 March, some 48 aircraft of the 721st Kokutai based at Kanoya headed out for Task Group 58.4. The central element of the enemy force was a flight of 'Betty' bombers under each of which was slung a rocket-powered Yokosuka MXY7 piloted bomb. Called *Ohka* ('cherry blossom') by the Japanese, this suicide craft was quickly dubbed with the similar-sounding Japanese name *Baka* ('screwball') by the Americans. But names could not hurt these air-launched one-way aircraft. In this particular instance, *Intrepid*'s fighters caught the 'Bettys' some 50 miles from the ship and shot down three of them and their destructive cargo and damaged three others. *Intrepid* escaped damage this time, but some of the enemy aircraft managed to get past the fighters and caused damage to the carriers *Enterprise* (CV-6), *Franklin* (CV-13) and *Yorktown*.

*Intrepid*-based aircraft flew support missions for the US Marine Corps invasion of Okinawa on Easter Sunday, 1 April 1945. In the days that followed, Air Group 10 participated in the destruction of some of the few remaining major combat ships in the Japanese Fleet. Lt-Cdr John Lawrence, skipper of VT-10, was awarded the Navy Cross for his actions on 7 April, during which he put a torpedo into the Japanese battleship *Yamato* (then under attack by several elements), then went on to sink single-handed an enemy destroyer and, despite heavy AA fire, put torpedoes into another destroyer. The second destroyer was finished off by Corsairs from VBF-10.

Late on the night of 11 April, *Intrepid* came under attack by a force of Japanese aircraft, but with the aid of radar and by using continuous automatic weapons fire, the carrier's gunners shot down the one enemy aircraft that came closest to the ship.

*Intrepid* was finally meeting – and beating – the Kamikaze threat. But her luck ran out on the afternoon of 16 April 1945. A major force of Kamikaze aircraft, including six *Ohka*-carrying 'Bettys' from the 721st Kokutai at Kanoya, were spotted heading for the carrier force.

The first to make a run on *Intrepid* was a 'Tony', which made a glide bombing run from 5,000yd directly ahead of the carrier. It was hit by the ship's gun fire at 3,000yd away from the ship and, at 1,500yd, it began to burn and then crashed into the water.

Two other suicide aircraft were also shot down in short order. Then, at 1335hrs, two Kamikazes came in from astern. One was stopped just

*Left:* Gunsight camera views of a 'Betty' carrying an *Ohka* suicide aircraft. The bomber was eventually destroyed by *Intrepid* aircraft./*US Navy*

*Top:* USS *Intrepid* (CV-11) trails smoke after first Kamikaze hit on 16 April 1945./*via Pete Clayton*

*Above:* Heavy smoke accompanies second Kamikaze hit on USS *Intrepid* (CV-11) on 16 April 1945. /*via Pete Clayton*

before it could hit the carrier and, indeed, crashed into the water off *Intrepid*'s starboard side. The other one, however, suffered only minor damage and, although trailing smoke, managed to make a vertical dive into the carrier's Number 3 elevator, on the aft part of the flight deck. It was the fourth time in 14 months that *Intrepid* had been hit by a suicide plane.

The Japanese aircraft hit with such force that the engine was driven into the flight deck and the Kamikaze's bomb penetrated to the hangar deck, where it exploded and set off a tremendous fire. Well experienced in such matters by now, the ship's damage control party put out the fire in 51 minutes and then quickly jettisonned some 40 aircraft that had been irreparably damaged by the explosion and fire.

Above decks, meanwhile, two 'Zekes' followed the carrier's rising smoke trail and came in from the starboard quarter to administer the coup de grace. Having none of that, *Intrepid*'s gunners nailed both aircraft just before they reached the ship. During the calm period that followed that last battle, work crews made temporary repairs to the flight deck so that Air Group 10's aircraft could be recovered aboard their own carrier.

Although USS *Intrepid* suffered some of the

heaviest damage of her wartime career during this Kamikaze attack, the high quality of temporary repairs was such that she could have continued operations. *Intrepid*'s efficiency would have been greatly reduced, however, so the Task Force Commander, Adm William F. Halsey, ordered the carrier back to Hunter's Point for complete repairs.

Back home in California, Air Group 10 was detached for temporary shore duty while *Intrepid* was in drydock. When repairs to the ship had been completed, on 29 June 1945 the Air Group rejoined *Intrepid* for what was to be their final war cruise to the Western Pacific.

Air Group 10's last offensive action came on 2 August, when fighters, bombers and torpedo aircraft attacked Wake Island, which had been seized by the Japanese early in the war, but which had been by-passed in favour of other more urgent targets. Now possessing the time and the means, *Intrepid*'s aircraft took a full measure of vengeance for the US Marine Corps ground and air units that had been so badly mauled during the original defence of Wake Island. Other units followed up the attack and *Intrepid* proceeded to Eniwetok, where she arrived on 6 August.

The final fury of World War 2 in the Pacific,